P9-DOD-658

Felt It! Stitch It! Fabulous!

Felt It! Stitch It! Fabulous!

Creative Wearables from Flea Market Finds

Katheryn Tidwell Bieber

A LARK/CHAPELLE BOOK

A Division of Sterling Publishing Co., Inc.
New York

A Lark/Chapelle Book
Chapelle, Ltd., Inc., P.O. Box 9255, Ogden, UT 84409
(801) 621-2777 • (801) 621-2788 Fax
e-mail: chapelle@chapelleltd.com
Web site: www.chapelleltd.com

Library of Congress Cataloging-in-Publication Data

Bieber, Katheryn Tidwell.
    Felt it! stitch it! fabulous! : creative wearables from flea market finds /
Katheryn Tidwell Bieber.
        p.   cm.
    Includes index.
    ISBN 1-60059-067-5 (hardcover)
    1. Felt work.   2. Felting.   3. Clothing and dress—Remaking.   I. Title.
TT849.5.B54 2007
746'.0463—dc22

                                2006029687

10 9 8 7 6 5 4 3 2 1

First Edition

Published by Lark Books, A Division of Sterling Publishing Co., Inc.
387 Park Avenue South, New York, N.Y. 10016

Distributed in Canada by Sterling Publishing, c/o Canadian Manda Group,
165 Dufferin Street, Toronto, Ontario, Canada M6K 3H6

Distributed in the United Kingdom by GMC Distribution Services, Castle Place,
166 High Street, Lewes, East Sussex, England BN7 1XU

Distributed in Australia by Capricorn Link (Australia) Pty Ltd.,
P.O. Box 704, Windsor, NSW 2756 Australia

ISBN 13: 978-1-60059-067-2
ISBN 10: 1-60059-067-5

For information about custom editions, special sales, premium and corporate
purchases, please contact Sterling Special Sales Department at 800-805-5489 or
specialsales@sterlingpub.com.

Editor: ELLEN PAHL
Design: KATHLEEN HOLMES
Photographer: STEWART O'SHIELDS
Illustrations: BERNADETTE WOLF
Editorial Assistance: DELORES GOSNELL
                    JENNIFER GIBBS

*This book is dedicated to my
father, Dale Lenwood Tidwell,
and to all of us who choose
to see the "gifts" in the
challenges life
offers us.*

Contents

Introduction

My eureka moment came as I was standing heartbroken in the laundry room. It was a scene you can probably relate to: a favorite wool sweater, a busy day, a large wash load, and...out came something fit for a teddy bear. I was miserable until it suddenly occurred to me that I was holding a lovely piece of felted fabric. Soft, warm material I could cut up and stitch into something new. Within days, I was back in the laundry room *purposely* shrinking dozens of thrift store wool sweaters and then turning their durable felted fabrics into zillions of great projects.

What I'd stumbled upon was a fabulous way to recycle old knits into smart, stylish wearables and accessories. With a few unloved wool sweaters, a washer and dryer, and some basic sewing skills, you, too, can start with ready-made knits and end up with hats, wraps, purses, and more, all created with a loving, handcrafted touch. The trick is in the magic of felting. Because felted knits don't unravel, they can be cut into any shape and sewn easily by hand or machine. And felted knits are so warm and soft that they're wonderfully touchable and perfect for countless projects.

Felted knits are very popular now, but the conventional way to make a felted item, such as a purse, is to knit a very large loose one and shrink it. This tends to be both time-consuming and (since wool yarn can be pricey) expensive. The approach I'll teach you is easy on the piggy bank, as it relies on back-of-the-closet or thrift store finds, and it's fast. If you're like me, you love the look of handcrafted knits and you take great pleasure in giving gifts you've created yourself rather than bought at the mall. But even if you have the knitting skills required, the magic ingredient that knitting requires—time—can be elusive. Every project in this book has that "hand-knit-with-love" look but can be completed in one afternoon.

Take a look at the Basics chapter first, and you'll learn how to do on purpose what you once did by accident (shrink sweaters). I'll show you how to cut the new fabric up into perfect fabric pieces, and we'll take a quick look at the very simple sewing skills you'll need to complete the projects in the book. All of the projects can be sewn by hand, though in many instances you can use a sewing machine for even more time-saving power. Then, I'll introduce you to ways to enhance your creations with needle felting and powdered drink–mix dyeing. I have lots of tips and tricks I've learned from years as a designer and fabric artist to share with you. And if you do knit, I'll show you how to combine knitting with fast felting to add an exciting new dimension to your work.

The 39 projects in this book range from a simple flower to embellish a favorite hat to a shoulder pack I've carried on trails and in trendy restaurants. Because you'll be finding your own knits to shrink, cut, and stitch, your creations will automatically be unique. And in no time you'll be able to take what you've learned here and dream up your own fabulous felted treasures.

Felting 101

What is felting, anyway? Technically speaking, felting occurs when you combine animal fibers (wool, fur, or hair) with moisture, heat, and agitation. Hot soapy water makes it easy for the fibers to slip around and become entangled. Agitation increases the fiber contact, and when the wool fibers have become so entangled that there is no more room for them to move, they form a firm, felted fabric that can be cut with scissors without unraveling.

Felting is actually a very old technique. Textile manufacturers of the Middle Ages felted (the technical term is *fulled*) fabric by scouring it in hot water with a cleaning agent, beating it or walking over it, then rinsing it in cool water. Today, many crafters knit extra large items and then felt them by agitating

What Is Fast Felting?

It begins with shrinking a pre-made sweater or other knit item on purpose, using soap and agitation to cause the fibers to interlock and become a felted fabric. You can then cut and sew this fabric like you would any other.

them in hot water by hand or in a washing machine. The fast-felting method this book will teach you saves both time and effort because you simply felt pre-made sweaters in a washing machine, cut them up, and then stitch together the felted fabric to create all kinds of new items.

Wool argyle sweater before felting

Wool argyle sweater after felting

Basket of Roses purse made from felted argyle sweater

What You'll Need

The supplies list for fast felting is fairly short and simple. Chances are good you already have many of the needed items.

Here are the essentials for felting:
- ❑ Wool sweater or other knit item
- ❑ Zippered lingerie bag or pillow protector
- ❑ Wool wash or mild dishwashing soap
- ❑ Washing machine
- ❑ Clothes dryer (optional)

Once you felt your pieces, you'll cut them apart, and—following the patterns provided—stitch the fabric to create the projects in this book. For this part of the process, the following supplies will come in handy:
- ❑ Chalk marker
- ❑ Measuring tape
- ❑ Scissors
- ❑ Hand-quilting thread and all-purpose thread
- ❑ Cotton darning or milliner's needle
- ❑ Tapestry needle
- ❑ Lining fabrics
- ❑ Sewing machine
- ❑ Iron
- ❑ Pins and pin-back fasteners
- ❑ Plastic canvas

As you gain experience and move beyond the basics, you may want to consider the following items for embellishing your projects to make them unique:
- ❑ Beads, bells, crystals, and other embellishments
- ❑ Buttons
- ❑ Embroidery floss
- ❑ Ribbons and yarn
- ❑ Vintage jewelry

No Moths Allowed

I have noticed from time to time that along with wool sweaters, I seem to have attracted a few moths. A good way to keep that from happening is to felt your sweaters soon after bringing them into your house. I also have learned that, in addition to cedar, lavender flowers do a good job of repelling moths too. I keep lavender flower sachets and bundles of dried flowers around my craft area. It keeps the moths away and I get to enjoy the aromatherapy!

Finding the Right Sweater

Since one of the joys of fast felting is saving time, I recommend using pre-knit wool sweaters (you can use scarves, too). Large and extra-large sweaters yield the most material, but keep your eye out for children's sweaters, too. They often come in delightful colors and are great for flowers and other projects. Another key element of my approach to fast felting is to keep it inexpensive. I do this by relying on castoffs and thrift store finds. Once you catch "fast felting fever" you will begin to find great sweaters everywhere.

When selecting a sweater to felt, start with one that's much larger than you want the final piece of fabric to be. Although most sweaters shrink up by about one-third, remaining about two-thirds of their original size, every sweater felts differently depending on the wool, how it was knit, and whether or not it was pretreated. It's possible that a loosely knit sweater that goes to your knees could end up toddler-size. Also, don't let color deter you from a great find—light colors can be changed by dyeing them (see Drink Mix Dyeing on page 16), and you can often use a less-than-favorite color of felt as an accent or in hidden parts of a project. Try using the material as a flower or leaf embellishment or as the soles on a pair of slippers.

If you are concerned that you may not have enough sweater fabric to complete a desired project, now is the time to be creative. Find another sweater or child's sweater in a complementary or contrasting color. Use a different color for slipper soles, purse handles, stripes, or mitten cuffs. Think of the little challenges that pop up along the way as opportunities, and you'll make fun discoveries, as quilters do when they "make do."

Some items are pretreated to prevent shrinkage. If this turns out to be the case with a sweater you've selected, don't despair—there are plenty of other ways you can use it. Cut it as desired, finish the seams with a zigzag stitch if you're worried about unraveling, and use it with a lining. Or make embellishments, such as the Rolled Victorian Roses (page 26).

Sweater Shopping Checklist

Not all items knitted of the same type of yarn will shrink and felt exactly the same way, but you can improve your chances of getting what you want by following a few simple guidelines:

- Select items that are 85 to 100 percent wool or other animal fiber for optimal shrinking and felting.

- When in doubt, look for sweaters with "dry-clean only" on their tags.

- Start with items that are significantly larger than you intend the felted piece of fabric to be.

- Select several sweaters in complementary colors, as though making a quilt. This will ensure that you have plenty of felted fabric for a project.

- Look beyond the design of a sweater and consider its potential as a flower, leaf, or background color.

- Be flexible—if a sweater doesn't felt the way you want, save it for a different project.

Different yarns and knits shrink at different levels

The Fast Felting Process

The washer and dryer are a felter's power tools, saving you the time and effort that hand-felting requires. For best results, shrink one or two like-colored sweaters at a time in a single load, because some colors may bleed onto others. Since the felting process can generate a lot of lint, place your sweaters in a zippered lingerie bag or pillow protector to protect your washer from excessive lint build-up. Although you may use your normal laundry detergent for the felting process, I've found that it can cause bleeding and other harsh effects. I prefer to use either a small amount of mild dishwashing soap or detergent specially formulated for woolens (sometimes called wool wash).

As you work, keep in mind that felting is not an exact science. Some yarns felt faster and shrink more than others. Typically, loosely woven wool sweaters tend to shrink up tight and thick while finer, more tightly knit sweaters may not felt as densely and may require more agitation time in the washer.

Loosely knit 100% wool shrinks and felts tightly.

Loose open stitch tightens and fills in.

Designs and patterns become softly muted after felting.

Angora shrinks and felts moderately, still retaining its soft drape.

Acrylic knits do not felt or shrink.

Fast felting takes from 20 minutes to an hour and a half, depending on how felted you want your sweater fabric. You may need to reset the agitation cycle on your washer as many as three or four times. Because it's best to check the progress of your fabric, a top-loading washing machine is ideal. A front-loading model requires you to run complete cycles and doesn't allow you to reset only the agitation cycle.

1 Place your sweater in a zippered lingerie bag or pillow protector.

2 Set your washer to the lowest water level and the longest cycle (mine is 12 minutes), and select the hot wash/cold rinse option. Add about 1 tablespoon of mild dishwashing soap or wool wash and start the washing cycle. I set my kitchen timer for 10 minutes.

3 Near the end of the agitation cycle, check the progress. The more the fabric is felted, the denser it is and the harder it feels. If the sweater isn't sufficiently felted, reset the washing machine for another agitation cycle. You can let it run the full cycle and then reset your machine; it will just take longer.

4 Once the sweater is rinsed and the cycle is finished, remove the felted sweater from the washer. If more shrinkage is desired, machine-dry it; otherwise, hang to dry. Occasionally when drying a sweater in the dryer, you may get some folds or creases; if so, simply steam them out with your steam iron set on wool.

Note for Knitters

If you want to knit items from scratch and then felt them, great! Just keep in mind that with fast felting, items can shrink as much as 50 percent or more, so be prepared to knit an item that is much larger than the final size of the project.

Off with the Buttons

When you fast felt sweaters with buttons and want to take advantage of the buttoned area, remove the buttons first. After felting, sew the buttons back on to align with the buttonholes so there won't be any gaps or bulges from uneven shrinking.

Cutting Fast Felt

You'll find patterns for the projects in the back of the book. To use a pattern, adjust it to the desired

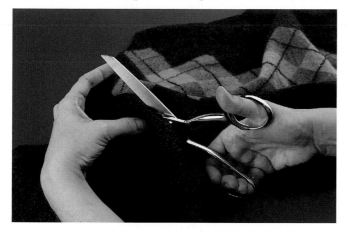

size by using the enlarge/reduce function on a photocopier or by using the gridded background to enlarge it by hand. Copy the pattern, cut it out, then lay the paper shapes on your felted fabric and pin them into place with straight pins. Seam allowances are included in all the patterns unless otherwise noted. Place the patterns to make the most efficient use of your felted fabric, or place them as directed in the project instructions. Some of the project instructions will tell you or show in illustrations exactly where to cut pattern pieces for

best use of fabric, or to include ribbing needed for the project. Others will tell you to cut sleeves off or cut ribbing off.

When you're sure you have fabric for all the pieces of your pattern, cut out the fabric using good-quality, sharp scissors—the kind our moms hid from us as kids so we wouldn't cut up paper, clay, and pipe cleaners with them! Don't be afraid—if you don't cut, you'll never make that fabulous purse!

A Note about Boiled Wool Sweaters

In my quest for sweaters, I often come across those that some people call "boiled wool." These are basically sweaters made from wool that is felted and then stitched into the final garment. Although you can shrink these further for a very thick felt, they are wonderful to use as is.

Cut your felted sweater apart at the seams, and spread the pieces out so you can see how much fabric you have to work with.

Sewing

If you can sew on a button, you have all the sewing skills you need for the projects in this book. You don't even need to have a sewing machine, although it can certainly be a great time-saver, and I use a sewing machine whenever possible.

There are a few things that will make your sewing go more smoothly. First, keep in mind that because felt is very thick, you'll usually need a larger-than-normal stitch length for best results—usually between ⅛" and ¼" long if you're hand-stitching. Select a needle that is long enough to travel easily through the thick felt. I like to use a milliner's needle or a cotton darner. Both are long and thin and have large, easy-to-thread eyes. Unless otherwise indicated, sew your seams ¼" from the edge of the felted fabric (this is the seam allowance).

It's important to match the color of your thread to your project for all parts that will show, such as a purse handle or the hem of a hat. Use cotton or a cotton-poly blend thread for most of the sewing in this book. For flowers, slippers, purses, and gathering, I prefer hand-quilting thread because it's nice and sturdy. This type of thread is a bit more expensive, but it is very strong. You don't need to have a lot of colors for flowers because the stitches don't show when they're in place; I simply use beige thread on light flowers and black on dark ones.

Piecing Felted Strips

There may be times when you need to piece shorter strips of felted fabric together to make one long strip for a purse handle or scarf. A good trick is to cut and piece the fabric on the diagonal. Butt the cut edges together and use small whipstitches to secure them together. When you roll it to make the handle, it will be less bulky at the seam.

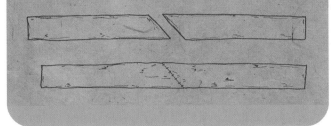

Sewing by Machine

If you're using a sewing machine, select a longer-than-normal stitch length or, if you want the stitched seam to have a little give, choose a short zigzag stitch. Be sure to brush away the lint from the bobbin case and other areas of your machine often; lint buildup can clog the works.

Sewing by Hand

There are a few stitches that I regularly use to complete fast felted projects. Each offers different advantages, so select which stitch to use according to the situation.

Hand running stitch. Use this for sewing ¼" seams. Make the stitches as small and close together as possible (figure 1). If the item will get a lot of use, you may want to stitch once, then go back again in the opposite direction to make two lines of stitches.

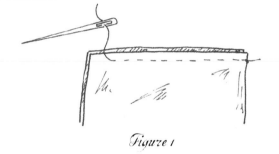

Figure 1

Hand-gathering stitch. Use a hand-gathering stitch (figure 2) when you will need to pull fabric into gathers. It is simply a longer version of the running stitch.

Figure 2

Whipstitch. Use this stitch when you need strength, when attaching a purse handle, for example. Insert the needle in one area and bring it out in another, as close as needed to hold two fabric pieces together (figure 3).

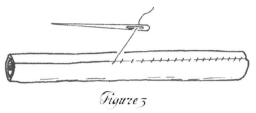

Figure 3

Blanket stitch. When the stitches will show, I often use a blanket stitch for its decorative look (figure 4).

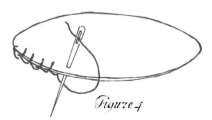

Figure 4

Tack stitch. Although this term can mean various things to different people, I define it as creating several stitches on the same spot for strength and permanence (figure 5).

Figure 5

Lining Fabrics

Some projects in this book are lined for added comfort and beauty. To keep my fast felted projects economical, I look no further than my scrap bag for material to use as linings. The red silk in the Basket of Roses Purse on page 56 came from scraps left over from my daughter's prom dress, and the purple satin lining the slippers on page 84 had been part of an old pirate costume. Vintage cotton from an old bedspread was repurposed as the lining for the Aran Isle Tote Bag on page 98. Be as creative in your search for lining fabrics as you are in your quest for sweaters to felt.

Special Techniques

Many of the projects in this book go from fine to fabulous when you take a little extra time to customize the project or embellish the felted fabric. If you knit, you can add your own knitted sections. If a pale felted sweater looks dingy or isn't the right color, change it with some dye. If a scarf or a hat needs some oomph, try some colorful needle-felted accents. The techniques aren't hard to master and can be as simple or as involved as you wish.

Knitting

Although the focus of this book is working with items you don't need to knit from scratch, I know some of you will *really* want to add a bit of your own knit work to your projects. For that reason, I've included a few projects that call for a little knitting. If you can knit, you'll be able to jump right into them. If you're ready to learn, check with experts at your local yarn shop and take a class; or refer to one of the many books written for beginning knitters. And if you like the look of the projects that include knitting, but don't have the time, interest, or skill to knit, look for sweaters with interesting features that you can cut off and use instead of knitting them yourself.

Drink-Mix Dyeing

Unsweetened powdered drink mix is an easy-to-use and inexpensive way to dye small pieces of felted fabrics. Best of all, this nontoxic option gives fabulous color and, as any mom can tell you, it's surprisingly colorfast. I pick up several packets of the same stuff

that's been around since I was a kid whenever they're on sale, but any brand will work if it contains vitamin C—the ascorbic acid enables the felt to take the dye. If you wish to dye more felted fabric, such as an entire sweater, you might need ten or more packets.

If you need to wash an item that has been dyed with this method, simply wash by hand in room temperature water with mild detergent. Roll the item in an old towel to remove excess water and then dry flat, out of sunlight, on another old towel.

Supplies

Felted sweater pieces

Scissors

Water

Glass container or glass pie pan

Small plastic spoon

Unsweetened powdered drink mix

Rubber gloves (optional)

Microwave oven

Old towels

Stick to Lights

For the most vivid color when drink-mix dyeing, start with white or ivory felted fabric. Start with gray, light blue, light green, or yellow fabric when you want a more muted effect. Of course, dyeing will have little, if any, effect on dark-colored fabric.

Instructions

You might want to cover your work area with newspaper or old towels. If any powdered drink mix gets on porcelain or tile, it is easily removed with a little bleach or other stain remover. Use rubber gloves if you don't want rainbow-colored hands. I don't use them because I love colorful fingers—it makes me feel very creative!

1 For flowers and leaves, cut 4" x 10" strips or 4" squares of felted sweater fabric and thoroughly wet the pieces by soaking them in lukewarm water for about 20 minutes.

2 Lay the fabric in a glass container or pie pan. Using a small plastic spoon, sprinkle the drink mix directly onto the wet fabric. If you want to blend more than one color together, add about ⅛" of water to the bottom of the pan.

To dye a whole sweater, soak it as instructed in step 1 and dissolve the drink mix in a large pot. Put the pot on the stove and place the sweater in it, having enough water to cover the sweater. Heat until just before the water boils. Then proceed to step 4.

If you want a rainbow effect, place the wet sweater in a large, microwave-safe bowl, sprinkle with different colors of powdered drink mix, and proceed to step 3.

3 Place the container or pie pan in the microwave for about 2 minutes on high. Carefully remove it and set aside until cool.

4 Rinse the dyed piece and blot with old towels. Discard the remaining water.

Overlap different colors of powdered drink mix to achieve unusual effects.

Pretty Edges

When you dye the fabric before cutting out shapes such as leaves and flower petals, the freshly cut edges will contrast with the dyed surfaces of the felt. This adds an interesting dimension to your projects.

Needle Felting

Needle felting is a spectacular way to embellish fast felted items. To do it, you use a specially designed needle to incorporate wool fiber, called wool roving, into the fabric. For those of you interested in expanding your creative horizons, I've included a few projects that use needle felting; however, it's not necessary to use this embellishment technique to create these projects. You could do embroidery or wool appliqué instead.

Unlike a sewing or an embroidery needle, a felting needle does not have an eye; it has a sharp point and tiny barbs along the length of the needle that cause the wool fibers to interlock with your base fabric. The fibers of wool roving become entangled with the fibers of the felted fabric, building the decoration into the fabric itself. With the recent introduction of felting tools that attach to a sewing machine, needle felting can be faster than ever before.

Needle felting by hand requires the use of a foam pad. Place it under your project to protect your work surface and the delicate felting needle. Although the felting needle should penetrate the fabric and go just ⅛" to ¼" into the foam, I recommend a piece of foam that is at least 3" deep for added security. (The needles are very sharp.)

Supplies

Felted wool (base fabric)
10" x 10" x 3" foam pad
Wool roving
Felting needle

Instructions

1 Place the felted wool base fabric that is to be embellished on the foam pad. Lay the wool roving across the base fabric.

2 Repeatedly jab the felting needle straight down through the roving and fabric until the roving is sufficiently incorporated into the base fabric. The action is like a chicken pecking at grain. Don't pick at the fibers or twist the needle.

3 If your design is larger than your felting pad, simply needle felt the area that does fit on the pad, lift that section of the design off of the pad, and lay the next area on the pad for felting. Continue until the entire design is complete.

Finding Foam

My favorite foam for felting projects is the dense, gray stuff that protects computers when they are shipped. If this isn't an option for you, a local upholstery shop may have foam scraps available. Craft stores may have foam inserts for pillows that will work. In a pinch, you can use the back of a sofa cushion, but I don't recommend this as a long-term option.

Timesaving Options

Speedier options to the traditional needle-felting method include using a hand-felting tool or a needle-felting attachment designed especially for use with a sewing machine. The hand-felting tool holds three or four felting needles and is used with the same pecking motion you'd use with one, enabling you to perform four times the work with every punch with the convenience and portability of a hand tool.

If you'd rather use a sewing machine, swap your ordinary sewing machine needle for a needle punch accessory tool. Like a hand-felting tool, a needle punch accessory tool groups three or four felting needles. To use it, you will need to exchange the sewing machine's faceplate with one that has an opening large enough to accommodate the attachment. Remove any bobbin and thread from the machine, arrange the wool roving on your felted fabric, place the fabric under the needles, and you're ready to go.

Blossoms: Roses and More in Bloom

"At the height of laughter, the universe is flung into a kaleidoscope of new possibilities."

—Jean Houston

"A kaleidoscope of new possibilities" is such a wonderful phrase. I love the idea of simply arranging and rearranging a few simple objects for a spectacular visual display. Create beautiful flowers with a few leftover pieces of felted fabric, powdered drink mix for some unexpected splashes of color, and a couple of vintage buttons or beads. Tie it all together with a needle and thread, add a little laughter, and see what possibilities unfold.

Because the projects in this chapter require very little fast-felted sweater fabric, they are ideal for using up scraps from other projects.

Angora Ribbing Rose with Bud

One of the easiest ways to create roses is with the ribbing of a sweater. The ribbing gives the petals a nice finished edge, so you can use it felted or unfelted. This technique is a good way to use ribbing from sweaters that didn't felt as much as you had wanted. As I collect and work with sweaters for various projects, I cut and save leftover ribbing if it has the potential to make a great flower.

Materials

Purple angora sweater, felted

Scraps of a green sweater, felted

Chalk marker

Needle and hand-quilting thread

Scissors

Vintage brooch

9 small beads

Pin-back fastener

Cutting

From the purple sweater, cut:

One 2" x 16½" strip of ribbing

One 2" x 20½" strip of ribbing

One 1" x 2" rectangle

One 2"-diameter circle

From the green sweater, cut:

Two 2½" squares

One 1½" x 5½" rectangle

Instructions

1 Starting ¼" from the cut end, divide the 16½" strip of sweater ribbing into four 4" sections, marking each section with a chalk marker. The last mark should be ¼" from the second cut end. Repeat this process with the 20½" strip of sweater ribbing, dividing it into five 4" sections.

2 To make a four-petal section from the shorter strip, run a hand-gathering stitch in a semicircular shape within each 4" interval (figure 1) using one strand of hand-quilting thread. Pull the thread slightly to form curved petals. Knot the thread to secure the gathers. Stitch the two short ends of the ribbing together. Repeat with the 20½" strip of ribbing to create a five-petal section.

3 Center the four-petal section over the five-petal section and stitch together. Stitch or glue a vintage brooch in the center and hand-stitch 8 beads around the brooch.

4 Cut two leaves from the green felted fabric squares, using the leaf pattern on page 108.

Overlapping slightly, stitch the leaves behind one side of the rose.

5 Roll the 1" x 2" piece of purple felt into a tube to make the rosebud center, and hand-stitch the raw edge (figure 2). Stitch a small bead to the center top of the bud. Lay the purple roll in the center of the green rectangle slightly above the top green edge. Fold the green rectangle around the purple bud (figure 3), and stitch to secure. Stitch the bud behind the rose, trimming off any excess green as needed.

6 Stitch the purple circle to the back of the rose and attach a pin-back fastener.

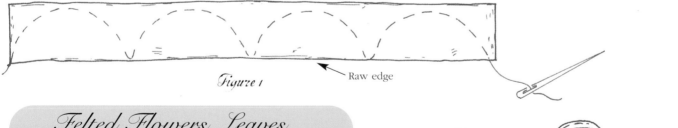

Figure 1

Raw edge

Felted Flowers, Leaves, & Accents

It's easy to make beautiful and colorful flowers by using even very small pieces of ribbing from a sweater. Simply cut a single petal section and run a hand-gathering stitch ¼" around the raw edges. Pull the threads slightly to form curved petals. Knot the thread ends together to secure, and trim. Use one section for a leaf, or make several and join them together for a flower.

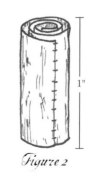

1"

Figure 2

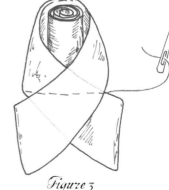

Figure 3

Ivory Angora Rose

According to legend, a dewdrop on a rose is a wishing gift from a fairy. Flick the dewdrop with your finger and your wish is bound to come true! Whenever I create roses, I remember this bit of fairy magic and add a vintage rhinestone or crystal to remind me of that magic dewdrop.

Materials

Ivory angora sweater, felted

Two 2½" squares from a green felted sweater

Chalk marker

Needle and hand-quilting thread

Scissors

Rhinestone button

19 light green crystals

Pin-back fastener

Cutting

From the ivory angora sweater, cut:

One 2" x 20½" strip of angora ribbing

One 2½"-diameter circle

One 2"-diameter circle

Instructions

1 Starting ¼" from the raw end of the sweater ribbing, divide the ribbing into five 4" sections, marking each one with a chalk marker. *Note: The last mark should be ¼" from the second raw end.*

2 Run a hand-gathering stitch in a semicircular shape within each 4" interval (figure 1). Pull the threads slightly to form curved petals. Knot the threads together to secure, and trim. Stitch the two short ends of the ribbing together.

3 Run a hand-gathering stitch around the edge of the 2½" ivory circle (figure 2). Pull up the gathers to make a yo-yo (figure 3). Knot the thread and trim. Flatten the circle, with the gathers in the center. Stitch a rhinestone button into this center.

4 Stitch the yo-yo to the center of the ribbing flower.

5 Cut two leaves from the green fabric squares, using the leaf pattern on page 108. Stitch the green crystals into the center of the green leaves. Overlapping slightly, stitch behind one side of the rose.

6 Stitch the 2" ivory circle to the back of the rose and attach a pin-back fastener.

Be Flamboyant

Experiment with flower centers to reflect your various moods. Add decorative rhinestone buttons when you're feeling flashy and fun, or attach a beautiful vintage brooch when you want a more elegant look.

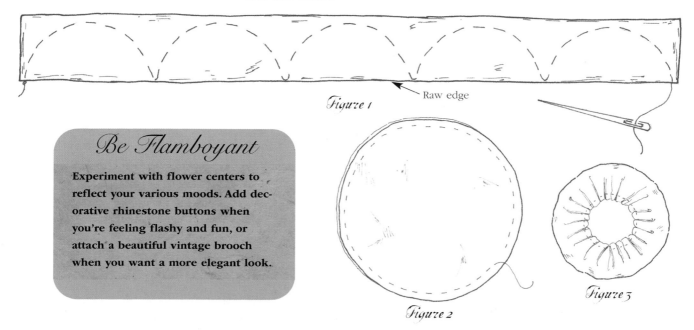

Figure 1 ← Raw edge

Figure 2

Figure 3

Rolled Victorian Roses

Rolled roses are easy to make and are a great way to use softer, fluffier felted sweaters and sweater scraps. Make them in clusters and use them to accent a jacket, sweater, purse, or hat. Or use one as a unique bow on a gift-wrapped package. These roses can also be made from those gorgeous silk and cotton sweaters in delicious, irresistible colors that I find in thrift stores. They don't felt, but they are perfect for creating these fabulous flowers.

Materials

Three 2" x 10" strips of violet felted sweater

Three 2½" squares of green felted sweater

One 2"-diameter circle of green felted sweater

Needle and hand-quilting thread

Scissors

Pin-back fastener

Instructions

1 Fold each 2" x 10" strip of felted sweater fabric in half lengthwise. Run a hand-gathering stitch around three sides of the strip, curving around the corners (figure 1). Pull the thread slightly at each end to gather the fabric, and then knot to secure it (figure 2).

2 Hold one end of the folded strip and roll it into a spiral to create the rose (figure 3). Stitch securely at the bottom. Make three roses.

3 Cut three leaves from the green felted squares, using the pattern on page 108. Arrange three roses together with three leaves behind them and stitch them together. Stitch the 2" green circle to the back of the flower and attach a pin-back fastener. Trim excess fabric from the green circle, if desired.

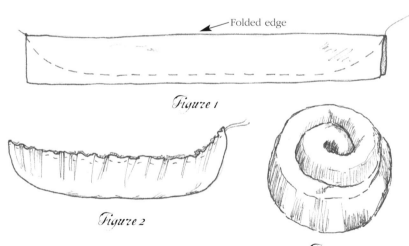

Folded edge

Figure 1

Figure 2

Figure 3

Change the Look

Use a matching thread color and take stitches along the folded edges of the petals of a finished flower at intervals of ½" to 1". Pull on the stitches to draw the edges down, creating a scalloped, more vintage look to the rose.

Twisty Lollipop Rose

Playful twists of pink and white remind me of the swirls of color on a big, twisty lollipop. Pin this brilliant bloom to a hat, bag, or coat lapel for a sweet, cheery touch. The fabulous color was produced by the drink-mix dyeing technique described on page 16.

Materials

Dye felted sweater pieces following the directions on page 16.

One 1¼" x 13" strip of dyed felted sweater

Two 2½" squares of green felted sweater

One 2"-diameter circle of green felted sweater

Scissors

Pins

8" x 10" piece of corrugated cardboard (size is approximate)

Needle and hand-quilting thread

Pin-back fastener or hair clip

Jazz It Up

Embellish your leaf shapes by adding sparkly beads or rhinestones.

Instructions

1 Cut ¼" off each side of the strip of dyed felted sweater to make a ¾" x 13" strip.

2 Pin one end of the fabric strip onto cardboard that has been laid flat on your work surface. Twist a section of fabric and roll it around the anchored end to form a spiral; insert straight pins into the spiral to hold it in place on the cardboard as you twist and roll (figure 1). Continue twisting and rolling until the entire strip has been used to form the rose. Secure the spiral with a few more straight pins so that you can detach it from the cardboard.

3 Hand-stitch the underside of the flower to secure each rolled spiral section to the next. Bring the end of the strip to the underside and stitch down.

4 Cut two leaves from the green fabric squares, using the leaf pattern on page 108. Overlapping slightly, stitch the leaves behind one side of the rose. Stitch the 2"-diameter green circle to the back, trimming as needed. Attach a pin-back fastener or hair clip.

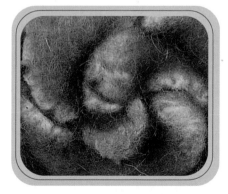

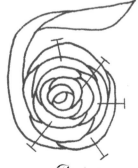

Figure 1

29

Emerson had it right, the earth does laugh in flowers, and these posies are a joy to make, especially when you celebrate your creative style by dyeing them beautiful shades of color.

Materials

Dye felted sweater pieces following the directions on page 16.

Three 2" squares of dyed felted sweater

Five 2½" squares of dyed felted sweater

One 2½" square of green (or dyed) felted sweater

One 1"-diameter circle of green (or dyed) felted sweater

Scissors

Needle and hand-quilting thread

Crystal bead

Pin-back fastener

Be on the Look-Out

Always keep your eyes open for sweaters in colors that would make good flowers and leaves— reds, pinks, turquiose, greens, etc.

Instructions

1 Cut three small petals and five large petals from the dyed fabric squares, using the petal patterns on page 108.

2 To form the center of the flower, fold one small petal in half lengthwise and stitch across the bottom to hold the fold. Attach a second small petal to the flower center by stitching the bottom edge of the petal to the flower center (figure 1). Layer the third small petal behind the first two, and stitch it to the flower center. Add the large petals in the same manner.

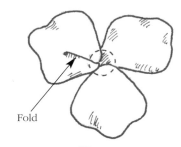

Fold

Figure 1

3 Stitch the bead in the center of the flower.

4 Use the leaf pattern on page 108 to cut a leaf from the green sweater square. Stitch it behind the flower. Stitch the 2"-diameter green circle to the back and attach a pin-back fastener.

Serendipity Rose Pins

I call these Serendipity Roses because their creation was a happy accident. I was toying with the idea of needle felting a few wisps of colorful wool roving to the center of each petal, and I found myself wrapping the roving around the petals instead, creating a totally new and unique look.

Materials

One 8" square of ivory felted sweater

One 4" square of green felted sweater

Scissors

Felting needle and foam pad

Wool roving: green, teal, and two shades of rose

Needle and hand-quilting thread

Pin-back fastener

Instructions

1 Using the Serendipity Rose petal patterns on page 109, cut three small petals and five large petals from the ivory felted sweater fabric. Use the leaf patterns on page 108 and cut one small leaf and two large leaves from the green felted fabric.

2 To needle felt the petals and leaves, place them one at a time on the foam pad. (Refer to page 18 for the needle felting technique.) Cover with a wisp of wool roving that is 2" longer than each petal or leaf; use teal or green roving for the leaves and rose for the petals. Use a small amount, thinly spreading the wisps to allow the petal or leaf to show through (figure 1). Needle felt the wool roving into the top and the bottom of each petal and leaf. Fold the extending wisps around to the back of each petal or leaf and needle felt them in place (figure 2). Needle felt a second layer of color to the petals and leaves.

3 To make the rose, take one small petal section and pinch it in half with your fingers along

the bottom edge. Stitch this folded edge closed. Wrap one petal around this center section and stitch in place at the bottom edge. Continue to wrap the rest of the petals around the center, overlapping each one (figure 3).

4 Arrange the leaves behind the rose and stitch in place. Attach a pin-back fastener.

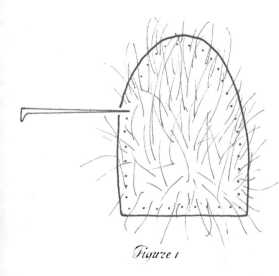

Figure 1

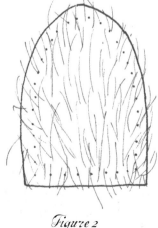

Figure 2

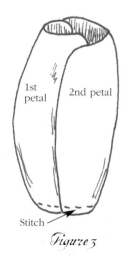

1st petal   2nd petal

Stitch

Figure 3

There are so many fabulous ways to use your felted flowers, and you can pin or sew them to just about anything. For this one, I combined the flower with a ready-made hat for a lovely and functional gift.

Materials

Two 4" squares of felted mauve sweater

One 3" x 4" rectangle of felted green sweater

Scissors

Needle and hand-quilting thread

Mother-of-pearl button, ⅞" or 1" in diameter

Purchased hat

Instructions

1 Cut two flower sections from the mauve sweater squares, using the inner and outer flower patterns on page 109. To make the inner flower petals, cut slits through the center of each petal as indicated on the pattern. Fold each slit right sides together and machine- or hand-stitch each slit closed from the reverse side to give the flower a little dimension.

2 Stitch the inner flower to the outer flower. Sew the button in the center.

3 Cut one leaf from the green rectangle, using the leaf pattern on page 109. Stitch behind the flower. Stitch the flower onto the hat.

Make More Than One

You can enjoy any number of different looks by simply exchanging the flower on this hat. Attach a Twisty Lollipop Rose (page 28) for some whimsical fun or an Ivory Angora Rose (page 24) for a retro look.

Cuddly and Snuggly: For the Little Ones

"Every child is an artist—the problem is how to remain an artist once we grow up."

—PABLO PICASSO

Living a creative life is all about play. For the fast felter, it's about playing with color, texture, and design, and trying new things like shrinking sweaters on purpose, or using three different colors to make one pair of elf boots. When you step into the playful, imaginative, and creative place where you can still see with the eyes of a child, you'll look at soft angora sweaters and see bunnies and teddy bears!

Teddy Bear Hat

What child wouldn't love a snuggly little bear hat to keep him or her warm on a blustery winter day? I used needle-felting to create the bear's face on this cheery, whimsical hat.

Materials

Brown sweater with ribbing, felted

Beige sweater, felted, or 4" x 5" piece

Scissors

Sewing machine (optional)

Needle and hand-quilting thread

Chalk marker

Felting needle and foam pad

Wool roving: beige, plum, maroon, and pink

Instructions

1 Use the hat pattern on page 110 and cut a front and back section, placing the bottom of the pattern along the ribbed bottom of the brown sweater. Cut two ear pieces from the brown sweater, using the ear pattern on page 110.

2 Cut one muzzle piece from the beige sweater. Place the muzzle on the hat front and zigzag stitch in place by machine, or stitch by hand.

3 Use a chalk marker to draw the face design from the pattern onto the front of the hat. Needle felt the design, following the instructions on page 18. For the eyes, use beige and plum roving; for the nose and mouth, use maroon roving; for the cheeks, use pink roving.

4 Lay a few wisps of pink wool roving on the center of the two ear pieces and needle felt them in place. Stitch a pleat in the bottom of each ear as indicated on the pattern. Place the ears on the bear's face where indicated, aligning the raw edges; the tops of the ears will point toward the bottom of the face (figure 1). The needle-felted sides should be facing each other. Stitch in place along the top of the hat.

5 Lay the hat front on the hat back with right sides together. Stitch together around the curved edges using a ¼" seam allowance. Clip the curves, trim the seams, if desired, and turn right side out. Fold the ribbing up and tack in place along the sides.

Figure 1

Elf Hat, Boots, and Ball

My son Tristan can be such an elf some days ... full of creative mischief and joy. I thought he needed a hat and boots to match the twinkle in his eyes. With the leftover felted fabric, I made a small, soft ball (see page 43) that's easy for little hands to grasp.

Elf Hat

Materials

Striped sweater with ribbing, felted

Scrap of bright green felted sweater

5" x 6" piece of teal felted sweater

Scissors

Needle and green hand-quilting thread

2 or 3 Beads (optional)

Instructions

1 Using the pattern on page 112, cut two hat pieces, aligning the bottom of the pattern with the ribbing at the bottom of the sweater. With right sides together, stitch around the raw edges, beginning at the bottom of the ribbing and ending at the ribbing on the other side. Clip the curves and trim the seams, if desired.

2 Turn the hat right side out. Roll up the ribbing to make the brim and tack in place. Twist the points together at the top of the hat and stitch together. Add beads at the top, if desired.

3 To make the butterfly, cut a 1½" x 1¾" rectangle of green felted sweater scrap. Roll this strip up tightly to make a 1¾"-long butterfly body, and stitch along the raw edge. Wrap the roll with thread ¼" from each end and again about ½" away from one end to give the appearance of a segmented butterfly body. Cut two upper and two lower wings from the teal felted sweater fabric, using the wing patterns on page 112. Stitch the wings to the underside of the body, and then stitch the butterfly onto the hat.

Beads, Bells, or Pompoms

You can add beads, bells, or other embellishments to the ends of this hat, but use soft pompoms and sew them on very securely when making it for a very young child. See page 78 for pompom instructions.

Elf Boots

Materials

Bright green sweater, felted

Teal sweater, felted

Magenta sweater, felted

Scissors

Sewing machine (optional)

Needle and hand-quilting thread

Pins

Wool or polyester stuffing (wool is preferred for warmth and comfort)

Embroidery needle and variegated embroidery floss

Instructions

1 Using the patterns on page 111, cut two boot soles from one color fabric. Cut four boot side sections, two each from two different colors.

Note: The printed pattern is sized for a baby. Enlarge the pattern by up to 133 percent for larger feet. Measure the child's foot and make sure the sole pattern is at least ½" longer than the foot measurement.

Other Options

Feel free to mix and match the colors for the boot sides. For a different look, stitch the boot wrong sides together and do not turn them. This allows the stitching to show on the outside of the boots.

2 Place two different color boot sections right sides together and stitch along the center back and center front by machine or by hand. Pin a boot sole to the bottom of each boot, matching the centers of the soles to the seams and using plenty of pins. Stitch around each sole. Baste by hand first, if desired. Turn the boots right side out and stuff a small amount of wool or polyester stuffing into the toe of each boot to hold the pointed shape.

3 Blanket-stitch around the top opening of each boot with six strands of embroidery floss. Add a few hidden stitches at the front and back seams of each boot to help the points of the boot openings hold their shape.

Elf Ball

Materials

Bright green sweater, felted

Blue sweater, felted

Striped sweater, felted

Scissors

Pins

Needle and embroidery floss

Wool stuffing

Instructions

1 Cut six pieces of felted fabric (two of each color), using the Elf Ball pattern on page 113. Pin two sections at a time wrong sides together, alternating the colors.

2 Stitch each pair together along the curved edge using the blanket stitch (see page 15) and three strands of embroidery floss. Pin the three double sections together to create a ball and blanket-stitch them together along the curved edges. Leave one section unstitched for stuffing.

3 Stuff the ball firmly with wool stuffing. Stitch the final section all the way up the ball to complete.

Plan Ahead

If you want to make the Elf Ball, the Elf Boots, and the Elf Hat with coordinating colors, lay out the patterns for all three projects at the same time to make sure you have all the fabric you need. I used parts of the same three sweaters for all of these projects.

The Ten-Minute Baby Hat

When a sweater doesn't felt as a tightly as you'd hoped, turn a negative into a positive by creating an extra-soft baby hat. Even better, this design can be created in as few as 10 minutes. Just imagine how many you and your friends could make in an afternoon! Donate a batch of them to a community shelter, and you'll feel the warmth of a job well done.

Materials

Ivory angora sweater or sleeve, felted

Scissors

Needle and hand-quilting thread

Instructions

1 If using a sleeve, cut an 8" x 9" tube—a 9" length of sleeve that is 8" wide (figure 1). This will create a tube that is 16" around. If using the body of the sweater, cut a 9" x 16" rectangle of the sweater, with the 16" length along the ribbing edge. Fold it in half and sew along the 9" side.

2 Roll up the end of the tube twice to make a 1½" brim. Tack the brim in place with small stitches (figure 2).

3 Turn the hat wrong side out and run a hand-gathering stitch ½" from the top edge with hand-quilting thread (figure 3). Pull the stitches tightly and knot to secure. Turn the hat right side out (figure 4).

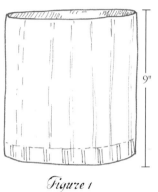

Figure 1

Figure 2

Figure 3

Figure 4

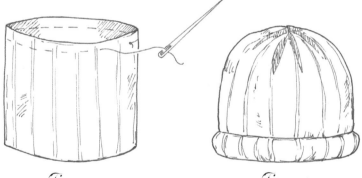

Make the Most of a Sweater

You can use many different parts of a sweater to make the Ten-Minute Baby Hat. Make hats from the sleeve, cowl neck, or bottom front and back ribbed edge of soft felted or unfelted sweaters. You can also use the main body of the sleeve or sweater without ribbing; simply zigzag the bottom raw edge, roll it up twice, and tack it in place at the sides.

Little Girl's Hat with Daisy

Imagine the look of delight on that special little girl's face when you give this charming hat to her. I made this hat from a lovely purple sweater using the same method as the Ten-Minute Baby Hat on the previous page. I added a flower and a few leaves, and voilà! I was done!

Materials

Purple angora sweater, felted or unfelted

One 2" x 7" piece of white felted sweater

One ⅜" x 4" piece of pink felted sweater ribbing

One 2½" x 5" piece of green felted sweater

Scissors

Needle and hand-quilting thread

Ladybug button (optional)

Instructions

1 Using the purple sweater, follow the instructions on page 45 to create the Ten-Minute Baby Hat, but use a piece that is 9" x 20" to make it larger for an older child.

2 Cut seven petals from the white felted fabric, using the flower pattern on page 116. Overlap the petals along the bottom side edges and run a hand-gathering stitch using hand-quilting thread to join them together along the bottom edge (figure 1). Pull the thread to gather and bring the ends together to create the daisy.

3 Twist the strip of pink ribbing and roll it tightly into a spiral. Stitch the bottom together to secure, using hand-quilting thread. Stitch the pink spiral to the center of the daisy.

4 Cut three green leaves from the green sweater, using the leaf pattern on page 116. Place the leaves around the back of the flower and stitch with hand-quilting thread to secure. Stitch the ladybug button to one of the leaves, and stitch the finished flower to the top of the hat.

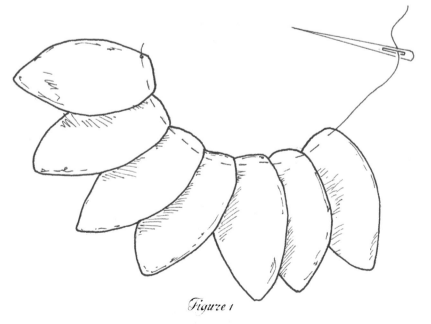

Figure 1

Together with the Ten-Minute Baby Hat (page 44), this bunny makes a lovely baby shower gift. The design was inspired by a hand-knit bunny that my son loved to play with as a toddler. Because I didn't have the skill or desire to knit something as tiny and delicate-looking as the original (on size 2 knitting needles), I devised a fast felted solution that takes me less than an hour with a few small pieces of fluffy angora fabric. Depending on the size of your sweater, you may find that these bunnies are so fast and easy to make that they almost reproduce themselves! I've made thirty from one large angora sweater and I'm still going!

Materials

Ivory angora sweater, felted or unfelted

Scrap of pink angora sweater, felted or unfelted

Scissors

Pins

Needle and hand-quilting thread

Polyester fiberfill or wool roving

Instructions

Note: The bunny's ears are not felted and could fray a bit. I think they look cute that way but you could also apply fray check, finish the edges with stitching, or cut them from felted fabric. Also, don't forget to save some blue angora scraps to make a few blue-tailed bunnies for the little Peter Rabbits out there!

1 Using the patterns on page 114, cut a bunny and ears from the ivory angora sweater. Cut a tail from the pink angora sweater.

2 Fold each leg in half diagonally with right sides together and pin. Use hand-quilting thread to sew each leg of the bunny pattern into a cone shape. Leave the tummy section open (figure 1).

3 Turn right side out and fill each leg with polyester fiberfill or wool roving; be sure to fill the front legs very lightly. Hand-stitch the middle underside section closed.

4 Run a hand-gathering stitch in a circle around the area that will become the head. Pull up the gathers tightly as you puff up and create a head shape (figure 2). Wrap this area twice with the thread to really tighten and separate the area. Knot to secure.

5 To make the eyes, thread a needle, and knot one end. Push the needle through one side of the head to the other side where the eyes would be. Repeat for a stronger indention and knot the end.

6 Fold the back legs forward and tack them to the underside of the bunny to look like haunches. Stitch the front paws together.

7 Tie a knot in the middle of the ear section (figure 3) and stitch this knotted section to the top of the head.

8 For the tail, fold the outside edge of the tail circle under about ¼" and run a hand-gathering stitch around the circle. Pull up the gathers tightly and knot to secure. Stitch the tail to the bunny.

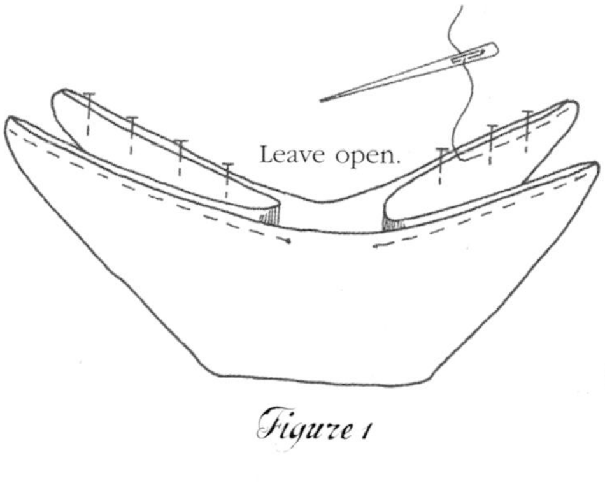

Leave open.

Figure 1

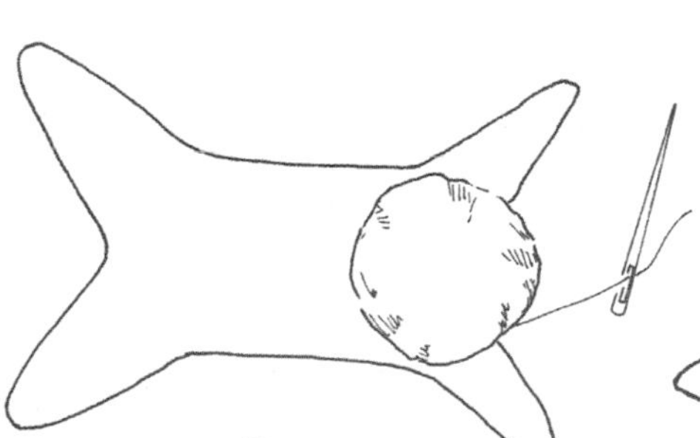

Figure 2

Figure 3

Children's Holiday Stockings

It has to be said … I am convinced that felting and stitching up wool sweaters to make fabulous things may be more addictive than chocolate! These stockings are the perfect example. I can't go by a thrift store now without popping in to look for something wonderful. I view them more as fabric shops; I'm always on the lookout for flower and rainbow colors that spark my creative spirit. It's easier than you might imagine to build a colorful felted sweater stash and begin making cheerful projects like these stockings.

Materials

Polka Dot Stocking
    Pink sweater, felted
    Scraps of fuchsia, green, and dark
        pink felted sweaters

Striped Stocking
    Striped sweater, felted
    Scraps of turquoise, green, orange,
        pink, and burgundy
        felted sweaters

Buttons

Argyle Stocking
    Turquoise sweater, felted
    Scraps of green, ivory, and
        burgundy felted sweaters

Pins

**Chenille needle and embroidery floss
    in coordinating colors**

Sewing machine (optional)

Needle and hand-quilting thread

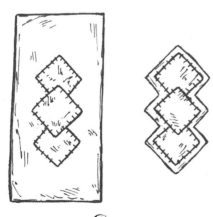

Figure 1

Instructions

1 Enlarge the pattern on page 121 by 200 percent, and then use it to cut a stocking front and stocking back from your sweater. Cut the striped sweater on the diagonal for a nice effect. Cut out embellishments from additional sweater colors using the patterns on page 121 (enlarge these by 200 percent, too). Cut one ¾" x 6" strip from the button front closure of a cardigan sweater (or any strip of felted fabric) to use as a stocking hanger.

2 To embellish the stocking, pin and blanket-stitch the polka dots or the argyle pattern before sewing the front and back of the stocking together. For the argyle pattern, lay the three diamond shapes in place on top of a green piece of felted fabric and blanket-stitch around them. Cut this unit out with approximately ¼" of green fabric showing all around (figure 1). Stitch that unit onto the stocking front. I used six strands of embroidery floss for all the designs. Wait until the side seams are sewn to stitch the stripes and partial polka dots along the edges.

3 Layer the front and back of the stockings wrong sides together. Machine or hand-stitch around the edges using a ¼" seam allowance.

4 Position and pin the stripes (if you're using them) and the toe and heel sections in place and blanket-stitch around them. Add the partial polka dots. This is done after stitching the side seams so that you don't have machine stitching over the designs along the edges.

5 Pin the decorations for the stocking top onto the front of the stocking, layer them together, and stitch them to the front of the stocking with a running stitch or blanket-stitch, keeping the back of the stocking free. Add a few buttons to the striped stocking for a fun accent.

6 Fold the ¾" x 6" strip of felted fabric in half and stitch securely to the top back of the stocking for a hanger, and you're done!

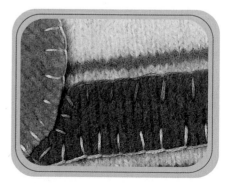

All Buttoned Up Stocking

This is a project that can be completed from start to finish in less than an hour when you take advantage of the boiled wool sweaters available in thrift stores. The stocking shown here was embellished with only a bit of embroidery around the edge; the rest of the design is just part of a lovely sweater, including the wonderful original buttons. Think of all the possibilities! If you want to felt the boiled wool sweater before using to make it even thicker, remove the buttons first. Sew them back on afterwards, aligning them with the buttonholes.

Materials

Boiled wool cardigan sweater

Scissors

Needle and embroidery floss

Instructions

1 Enlarge the stocking pattern on page 121 by 280 percent and cut it out of paper.

2 Lay the pattern upside down on the sweater (figure 1) so that the bottom ribbed edge of the sweater will be the top of the stocking and the curved sleeve seam will fall in the toe area. Align the buttons slightly off center toward the back of the stocking (to look more like a boot). Pin the pattern and cut out the stocking front and stocking back. Cut off the sleeve ribbing for a hanger.

3 Using six strands of embroidery floss, blanket-stitch around the sides and bottom of the stocking. Stitch the stocking loop hanger to the top back of the stocking with embroidery floss.

4 Embellish the stocking as desired with more embroidery, wool felt designs, vintage lace, or jewelry. Or just enjoy the design of the sweater as I did!

Stocking hanger

Figure 1

On the Go: Beautiful Bags & Totes

"Let the beauty of what you love, be what you do."

—RUMI

More than just about anything else, I love working with my hands. The connections among heart, hands, and creative spirit bring me a peace and joy that add depth to my life. Since I usually have more than one creative project going, I like to bring them with me on my daily adventures, meaning I need plenty of purses, handbags, and totes. The ones in this book are a wonderful combination of form, function, and style. Not only are they beautiful, but they also allow you to have a project at the tip of your fingers, ready to go when you are.

Basket of Roses Purse

Argyle sweaters are some of my favorites to work with. I love the combination of soft flowers with the graphic design. The roses on this project are perfect for using those bright colored silk, cotton, or acrylic sweaters that don't shrink or felt like wool. I lined these purses with leftover fabric from my daughter's prom dress. The instructions are written for a bold black and white purse with red roses, but you can create a much softer look by substituting a light gray and pink argyle sweater and pink roses.

Materials

Argyle sweater, felted

Red sweater, felted

Scraps of two green felted sweaters

Scissors

Sewing machine (optional)

Needle and thread

Pins

Plastic canvas

⅓ yard silk or other lining fabric

Instructions

1 Cut one purse front, one purse back, and one purse bottom from the argyle felted sweater (figure 1), enlarging the pattern on page 115 to the size of your choice. Cut two 1½" x 14" strips from the felted sleeve for the purse handles (figure 2).

2 With right sides together, stitch the purse front and back at the sides by machine or by hand. Turn the top edge of the purse down 1" to the inside and hand-stitch. Pin the purse bottom to the purse, right sides together, and stitch.

3 Cut a piece of plastic canvas the size of the purse bottom (minus the seam allowance) and hand-stitch it to the inside bottom of the purse for support. Turn the purse right side out.

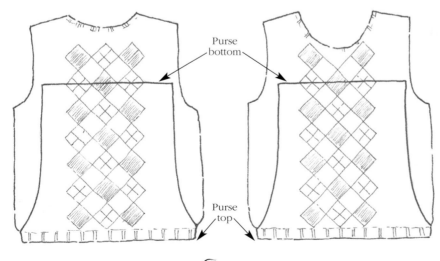

Purse bottom

Purse top

Figure 1

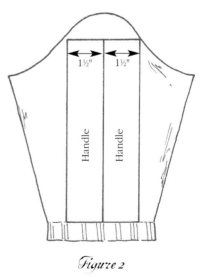

1½" 1½"

Handle Handle

Figure 2

Basket of Roses Purse

4 Tightly roll each handle strip lengthwise and hand-stitch along one long edge (figure 3). Whipstitch the handles in place on the inside-front and inside-back edges of the purse.

5 Cut two pieces of lining fabric using the purse pattern and one piece of lining fabric using the pattern for the purse bottom. With right sides together, stitch the lining pieces together at the sides. Pin the purse bottom to the sides, right sides together, and stitch in place. Clip the curved seams, if needed. Turn the top edge of the lining down ½" and pin in place. Insert the lining into the purse, having the right side out inside the purse. Hand-stitch in place along the top edge.

6 Make rolled roses by cutting three 3" x 17" strips from the red felted sweater. Fold each strip of fabric in half lengthwise and run a hand-gathering stitch along the three open sides of the fabric strip (figure 4). Pull the thread slightly and secure it with a knot (figure 5). Roll the strips up into a rose and

stitch to secure (figure 6). Stitch three roses to the front of the purse. See Rolled Victorian Roses on page 26 for additional details, if needed.

7 Cut ten green leaves from the green felted scraps, using the leaf patterns on page 115. Tuck and arrange the leaves behind the roses and stitch in place.

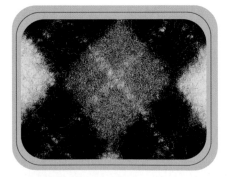

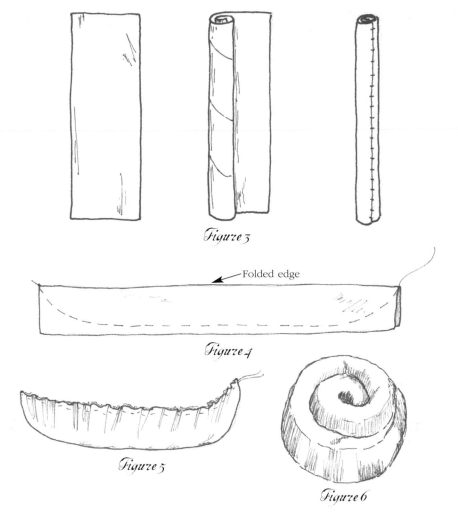

Figure 3

Folded edge

Figure 4

Figure 5

Figure 6

Big
Beautiful
Tote

Big Beautiful Tote

This bag began as an enormous hand-knit sweater from Peru. I felt a little guilty about making it into something else until I accepted the fact that no one I knew would consider wearing a sweater that was now out-of-style and also a little on the scratchy side. After felting the sweater, the highly detailed and colorful designs became subtler and softer, giving the sweater new life as a tote for knitting projects.

Materials

Dark teal sweater, felted

Extra large dark blue patterned sweater, felted

Scissors

Chalk marker

Plastic canvas

Pins

Needle and hand-quilting thread

Sewing machine (optional)

Polyester fiberfill or wool roving

⅝ yard fabric for lining

3 silk or vintage velvet leaves

1½"-diameter vintage button

Instructions

1 Cut two 4" x 26" strips from the sleeves of the dark teal felted sweater for handles (figure 1). Set aside.

2 Draw a straight line across the blue felted sweater just below the arms, using a chalk marker (figure 2). Cut the sweater along this line and set aside. *Note that the ribbed edge will be the top of the purse.* Measure and cut a

Easy Stuffing

Use chopsticks or the handle of a wooden spoon when stuffing the tube.

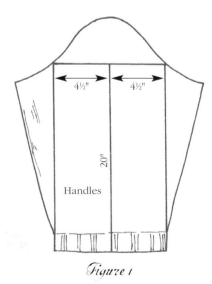

Figure 1

purse bottom from one sweater sleeve using the Purse Bottom Formula at right. Cut a piece of plastic canvas the same size minus the seam allowance.

3 Pin the purse bottom to the purse, right sides together, and stitch. Hand-stitch the plastic canvas to the inside bottom of the purse for support.

4 Fold the ribbed purse top down along the outside of the purse. Hand-stitch the ribbing in place. *Note: If the ribbing is all one color, it makes a nice contrast to the patterned design of the sweater.*

5 To make the handles, fold each handle strip in half, right sides together, and machine-sew down the long side and across one short end. Turn right side out and

stuff with wool or polyester stuffing to help them hold their shape. Whipstitch the handles in place securely on the inside front and inside back of the purse.

6 To create the purse lining, cut two pieces of lining fabric the same length and width as the purse. With right sides together, stitch the fabric pieces together at the sides. Cut a purse bottom, pin, and stitch in place. Clip the curves along the bottom. Turn the top edge of the lining down ½". Pin the lining in place, right side out, inside the purse. Hand-stitch in place.

7 Stitch three decorative silk leaves and a vintage button to the front of the purse for a nice finishing touch.

Purse Bottom Formula

To make a purse bottom to fit your purse, create a rectangle based on the sweater size and how wide you want the bottom of your purse to be. I typically make purse bottoms that are 3" or 4" wide. To find the size of the rectangle you need, follow the steps below.

1. Measure the distance across the bottom of the sweater when it is lying flat.

2. Decide how wide you want the purse bottom to be. That distance is the width of the rectangle.

3. Subtract the width in step 2 from the distance across the sweater in step 1; that number is the length of the rectangle.

For example, if the width of the sweater bottom is 14" and the desired purse bottom width is 4", the size of the rectangle for the purse bottom would be 4" x 10". As another example, if the width is 18" and the desired purse bottom width is 6", the purse bottom would be a 6" x 12" rectangle.

4. Create a paper pattern using this measurement, round the corners slightly if desired, and add a ¼" seam allowance all around. Use this pattern to cut the correct-size purse bottom.

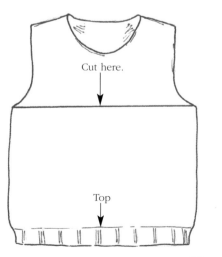

Cut here.

Top

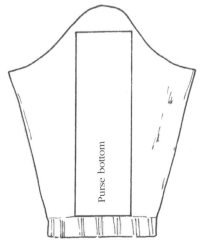

Purse bottom

Figure 2

Day-to-Evening Shoulder Pack

Nothing beats a versatile shoulder pack. I like having a bag that can go with me through the travels of my day and still end up at a nice restaurant without looking shabby. I think this one fills the bill!

Materials

Purple sweater, felted

Dark purple sweater, felted

Scissors

Pins

Needle and hand-quilting thread

Plastic canvas

⅝ yard lining fabric

24" of ¾"-wide decorative trim

Vintage brooch

Instructions

1 Cut off the sleeves of the purple felted sweater. Cut the shoulders off the sweater at an angle (figure 1). Cut one sleeve open at the seam, and lay the felted fabric flat. Measure the bottom of the purple sweater and use the Purse Bottom Formula on page 61 to make a pattern for the bottom of the pack. I made a 6"-wide bottom, but you could make it 4" or 5", if you prefer. Cut the bottom section from this sleeve (figure 2).

2 Cut the ribbing off the bottom of the purple sweater. From this, cut a 2" x 14" strip and set aside for the flower.

3 Cut one pack flap from the dark purple felted sweater sleeve (figure 3), enlarging the pattern on page 113 as needed.

4 From the dark purple sweater, cut one 3" x 10" strip for the handle and two 3" x 13" strips for the shoulder strap.

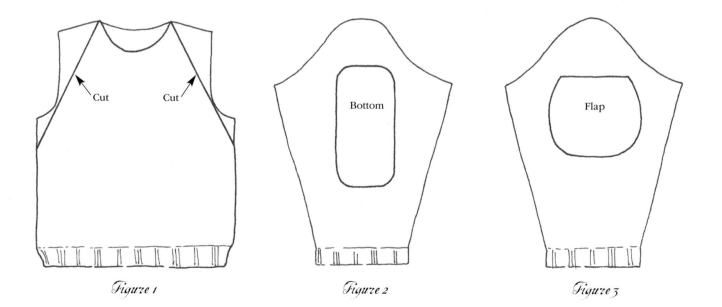

Figure 1   *Figure 2*   *Figure 3*

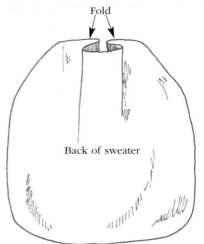

Fold

Back of sweater

Figure 4

5 Make two folds (¾" to 1") along the top on the back of the purple sweater, to create a pleat. Adjust the pleats as needed until the measurement across this piece is 6½", to match the length of the flap later on. Pin and sew the pleat in place (figure 4).

6 Stitch each side sleeve opening closed. Stitch the bottom of the pack to the bottom of the sweater with right sides together. Cut a piece of plastic canvas using the pack bottom pattern, but take off the ¼" seam allowances all around. Sew the plastic canvas to the pack bottom.

7 Cut two pieces of lining fabric each the length and width of the main body of the shoulder plus ½" seam allowances on the sides. Cut one piece of lining the length and width of the purse bottom and cut a lining for the flap.

8 Sew the two sides of the lining, right sides together. Pin and sew the lining bottom to the sides. *Note: You may need to gather the sides of the lining fabric along the bottom edges slightly to make it fit perfectly around the bottom section.*

9 Place the lining inside the bag, right side out. Pin the top edges of the bag and bag lining together. Fold the top edge of the lining (so that the raw edge does not show) down ½"; the top fold should be even with the top edge of the bag. Pin in place and hand-stitch. Hand-stitch the decorative trim over the stitching.

10 Lay the flap and flap lining right sides together, and stitch three sides together. Turn right side out and hand-stitch the opening closed. Stitch the flap to the top back of the bag.

11 Run a hand-gathering stitch along the cut edge of the 2" x 14" strip of ribbing. Make a rosette following the instructions below. Attach the vintage brooch to the center and stitch the finished rosette onto the shoulder pack front flap.

12 To make the shoulder pack handle, roll the 3" x 10" strip and whipstitch the outside raw edge of the roll (figure 5). Whipstitch the handle to the top back of the bag on either side of the flap.

13 To make the shoulder strap, stitch the two 3" x 13" strips together on the diagonal (see page 14) to form one 3" x 26" strip. Fold the sides of the strip over so that one side is overlapping the other. Whipstitch the outside raw edge (figure 5). Stitch one end of the strap to the top center back of the shoulder pack and the other end to the bottom center back.

Figure 5

Making Ribbing Rosettes

Make an easy rosette by running a hand-gathering stitch along a length of ribbing and pulling the threads tightly to gather. Bring both ends together and stitch, forming a gathered circle. Knot to secure. Add a vintage button or brooch in the center.

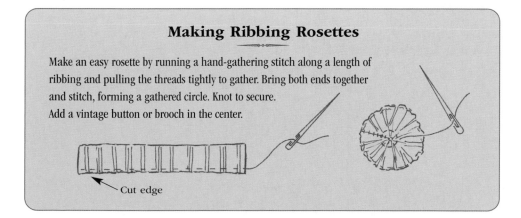

Cut edge

Over-the-Shoulder Bag

The shape of this bag makes it easy to fill, and there is plenty of room for a knitting project, book, or journal. Toss in several items, throw it over your shoulder, and you're ready to head out to run daily errands or, better yet, relax at a park or river and treat yourself to some creative downtime.

Materials

Red sweater, felted

Scraps of green felted sweater

Scissors

Pins

Needle and hand-quilting thread

¾ yard lining fabric

Plastic canvas

Button or vintage brooch

5 or 6 beads

Instructions

1 Cut the sleeves off the red sweater. Cut the neck and shoulder portions off the sweater, squaring off the neck (figure 1). Cut open the seams of the sleeves, and lay the sweater fabric flat. Cut two straps and a 4"-diameter circle for the purse bottom from the sleeves (figure 2). Cut the ribbing off both sleeves and save to make the flower.

Pack an "Inspiration Picnic"

Fill this bag with some goodies and toys to inspire your creativity . . . a small watercolor set, knitting needles and a colorful ball of yarn, your favorite book or journal and pen or crayons, and a bottle of spring water for refreshment. Go outside, find a quiet spot under a tree, and you're certain to be inspired to create.

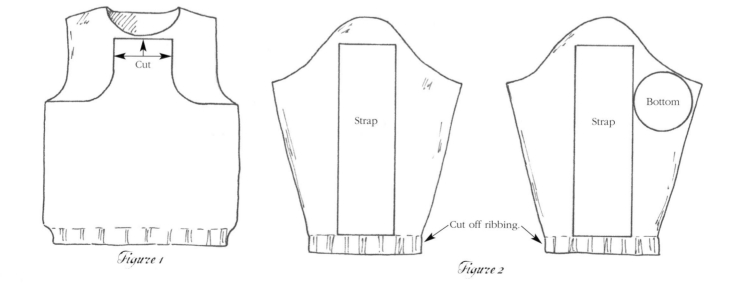

Cut

Figure 1

Strap

Strap

Bottom

Cut off ribbing.

Figure 2

2 Pin a purse strap to the front and back of the purse, right sides together, and stitch in place. Do not stitch the straps together at the top yet (figure 3).

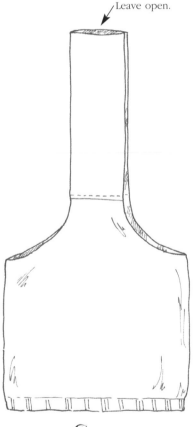

Leave open.

Figure 3

3 Cut two pieces of lining the same size as the purse body sections. With right sides together, sew the side seams. Cut a 4"-diameter circle from the lining for the purse bottom.

4 Turn the lining inside out and slip it over the purse body. Pin the lining to the purse straps and purse opening, right sides together, and stitch. Trim and press the seams. Pull the lining back over the purse and tuck the lining inside the purse body. Hand-stitch the top strap sections together.

5 To make the lining bottom, cut a 3½"-diameter circle from the plastic canvas and set aside. Run a hand-gathering stitch around the 4" lining circle and pull up the gathers slightly. Place the plastic circle inside the 4" circle and pull up tightly on the threads (figure 4). Stitch to secure. Run a hand-gathering stitch around the bottom opening of the purse lining and pull up the gathers. Center and pin the lining circle (with plastic canvas inside) to

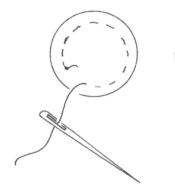

Figure 4

the bottom of the lining and hand-stitch in place (figure 5). Repeat this process for the felted purse bottom, using a 3½"-diameter plastic canvas circle and the 4"-diameter felted circle (figure 6).

6   To make the decorative floral accent, stitch the sleeve ribbing pieces together to form one long strip, approximately 14" long. If it is longer, you can trim it or use a longer length to make a fuller flower. Run a hand-gathering stitch around the bottom edge of the ribbing strip. Pull up the gathers, bring the ends together, and stitch. Stitch or glue the button or vintage brooch to the center. Cut three leaves from the green felted fabric using the leaf pattern on page 108, and stitch glass beads to their centers. Stitch the leaves behind the flower and attach the flower to the purse at the base of the shoulder strap or on the side of the purse for another look.

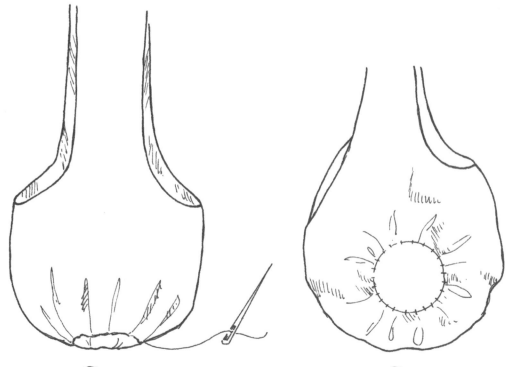

Figure 5   *Figure 6*

Retro Neon Handbag

Use your firmly felted sweaters in bright splashy colors to create this handbag.
It has just the right amount of flair when you're in an artsy mood.

Materials

Pink sweater, felted

Green sweater, felted

Scraps of turquoise felted sweater

Scissors

Pins

Needle and hand-quilting thread

Crystal bead

Dark green wool roving (optional)

Felting needle and foam pad (optional)

Cutting

From the pink felted sweater, cut:

Four 5½" x 9" rectangles for the purse front and back

From the green felted sweater, cut:

Two 4" x 14½" strips for purse sides

Four 2¼" x 16" strips for handles

Instructions

Use a scant ¼" seam allowance when sewing the purse pieces together.

1 To create the front of the purse, sew two 5½" x 9" pink rectangles, wrong sides together, along the 9" sides. Repeat to create the back of the purse. Round off the lower corners of the purse.

2 To make the purse sides and bottom, sew together the two 4" x 14½" strips of green felted fabric along the 4" ends wrong sides together. Pin the bottom and side sections to the purse front, right sides together, and stitch (figure 1). Repeat for the purse back.

3 To make the first handle, stitch together two of the 2¼" x 16" green strips along the 2¼" edge. Roll each handle and whip-stitch the outside raw edge. Repeat to create the second handle.

4 Before attaching the handles to the purse, roll each end up into a spiral (figure 2). Hand-stitch the spirals in place, then whip-stitch the handles to the purse as shown in the photo on the opposite page. Note: You can embellish the handle by cutting two narrow strips from the turquoise fabric and hand-stitching the strips to the inside of each handle.

5 Using the flower pattern on page 109, cut the flower shape from the turquoise felted sweater (do not cut slits in the flower for this project). Stitch a bead to the flower center. Using the leaf pattern on page 117, cut two leaves from the green fabric. If desired, needle felt a few wisps of dark green wool roving to the leaves using a felting needle and foam pad (see page 18). Stitch the flower and the leaves to the front of the purse.

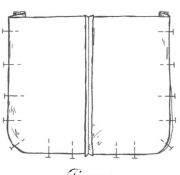

Figure 1

Figure 2

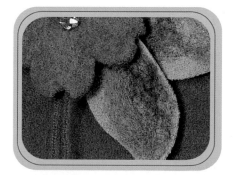

Warm & Cozy: Hats, Wraps, and More

"Write it on your heart that every day is the best day of the year."

—RALPH WALDO EMERSON

On a daily basis, someone in my home is bound to exclaim, "Happiest Moment!" This is verbal shorthand for embracing each moment as if it were the happiest moment of our lives. I used to think that we were allowed only a few of those moments—falling in love, having a child, or accomplishing a tremendous goal like climbing Mount Everest. Now I realize that returning a loved one's smile, enjoying the fragrance of sweet peas blossoming in your garden, or giving handmade gifts like the ones in this section fill my life with happiest moments.

8"

74

Winter Wonderland Set

This wonderful wrap and hat set is easy to make and luxurious to wear. Both pieces are made from soft angora. The scarf's lettuce-leaf edges take far less time to make than you'd think.

Wrap

Materials

Hip-length ivory angora sweater, felted or unfelted

Scrap of ivory felted sweater

Scraps of green felted sweater

Scissors

Pins

Needle and hand-quilting thread

1 large pearl

5 small beads

Pin-back fastener

Note: The lettuce-leaf edging technique relies on having a fairly stretchable fabric, so use it on minimally felted or unfelted sweaters to achieve the desired result.

Instructions

1 From the ivory angora sweater, cut four 8" x 33" strips with ribbing along the 8" edge (figure 1) and one 2" x 14" strip of ribbing.

2 Lay two of the 8" x 33" strips of ivory angora fabric end to end, with the ribbing on the outside ends (figure 2). Sew along the 8" length with right sides together. Repeat for the other two strips. Open the strips and pin them together on the long edge, matching the center 8" seams. Stitch with right sides together. I stitched these seams with a small zigzag stitch so they would have more give. Open and press the seams, if necessary.

3 Finish the outside edges with the lettuce-leaf technique: Using the zigzag setting on a sewing machine, a short stitch length, and a very narrow stitch width, sew along the edge of the wrap (figure 3). As you sew, stretch the edge of the fabric to create a ruffled effect similar to the edge of a lettuce leaf. You might want to practice on a scrap of fabric first.

4 Make an Ivory Angora Rose using the ribbing (page 24). Stitch a pearl in the center and small beads around the pearl.

5 Cut a five-petal felted flower from the ivory felted sweater scrap, using the flower pattern on page 116. Center the Ivory Angora Rose on the five-petal felted flower and stitch to secure, using hand-quilting thread. Cut two leaves using the pattern on page 116 from the green felted scraps. Stitch one leaf to each side of the flower. Stitch a pin-back fastener to the flower and pin it on one end of the wrap.

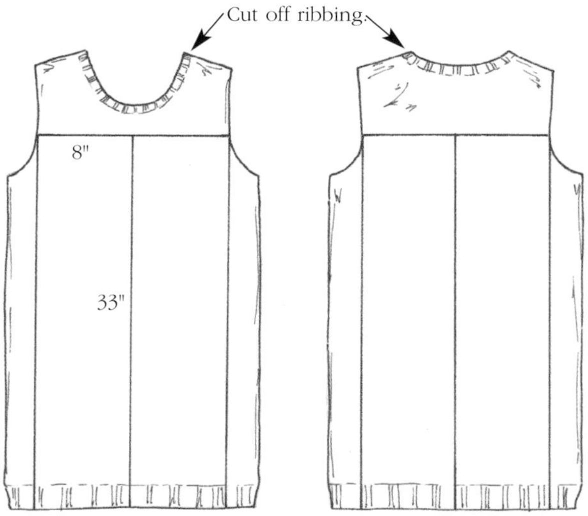

Cut off ribbing

8"

33"

Figure 1

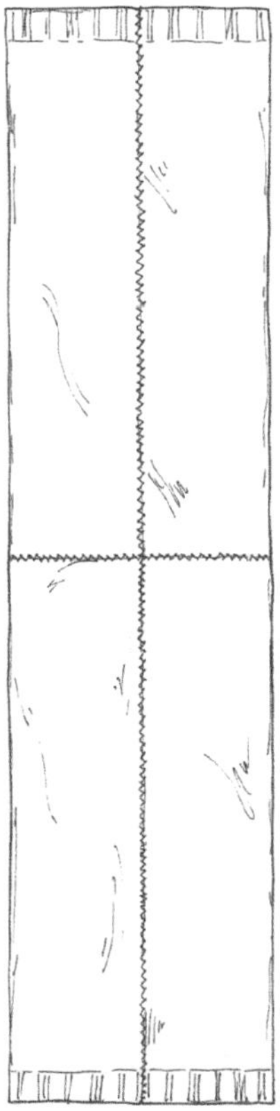

Figure 2

Figure 3

Winter Wonderland Set

Hat

Materials

Ivory angora sweater, unfelted

Scraps from an ivory felted sweater

Scraps from a green felted sweater

Scissors

Needle and hand-quilting thread

1 large pearl

5 small beads

Instructions

1. Cut two 7" x 11" pieces with ribbing from the ivory angora sweater; use the sleeves if possible (figure 1). If not, you can use a front and back, or use just a front if it is at least 22" wide (cut one piece 7" x 22"). Cut a 2" x 14" strip of ribbing.

2. Stitch together the two 7" x 10" pieces of ivory angora, along the 7" sides, right sides together.

3. With the ribbing at the bottom, run a hand-gathering stitch along the top edge of the hat with hand-quilting thread. Pull the stitches tightly and knot to secure. Turn right side out.

4. Make an Ivory Angora Rose (page 24) using the strip of ribbing. Stitch the pearl in the center and small beads around the pearl; it's not necessary to make the yo-yo center. Do not attach the leaves yet.

5. Cut a five-petal felted flower from the felted ivory scraps, using the flower pattern on page 116. Center the Ivory Angora Rose on the five-petal felted flower and stitch to secure. Cut two leaves from the green felted sweater scraps and stitch them to one side of the flower. Stitch the flower securely to the hat.

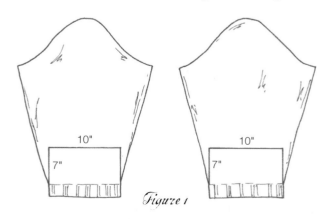

10"

7"

10"

7"

Figure 1

Warm Fuzzy Hat and Mittens

Warm Fuzzy Hat and Mittens

My daughter, Skylar, learned to make "warm fuzzy" pompoms at school and often leaves one as a calling card after performing a kindness. She taught me how to make them and I just had to top a hat with one to pass on warm fuzzy feelings.

Hat

Materials

Rose sweater, felted

Striped sweater, felted

One 2½" x 22" strip of ivory felted sweater ribbing

Scissors

Needle and hand-quilting thread

Pins

Wool yarn

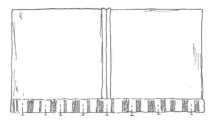

Figure 1

Cutting

From the rose felted sweater, cut:
Two 9" x 11" rectangles

From the striped felted sweater, cut:
Two earflaps from the sleeve
(pattern on page 117)
Two 2½" x 14" strips

Instructions

1 With right sides together, sew the two 9" x 11" rose felted pieces together along the 9" sides.

2 Pin the ribbing to the bottom edge of the hat, pinning the right side of the ribbing to the wrong side of the hat so that the ribbing will hide the seam when the edge of the hat is flipped up (figure 1). Sew the seam. With right sides together, stitch the side seams of the hat, including the ribbing. Trim the seam, if desired, and turn right side out.

3 Hand-stitch the earflaps in place on either side of the hat. Try the hat on first to determine the best placement of the flaps. If desired, line the flaps with a layer of felted wool before stitching them to the hat: layer the flap and lining right sides together, stitch around the curved sides, and turn them inside out.

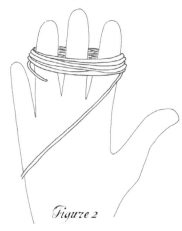

Figure 2

Figure 3

Figure 4

4 To make the hat straps, roll each of the two 2½" x 14" strips of striped felted fabric along the long edge and whipstitch along the outside raw edge. Leave one end slightly unrolled. Stitch the unrolled end of the tie to the bottom center of an earflap. Repeat to complete the second earflap.

5 Run a hand-gathering stitch 1½" down from the top edge of the hat. Pull the stitches tightly and knot to secure.

6 To make the pompom, spread apart your fingers. Wrap yarn around three fingers at least 50 times (figure 2). Tie the lengths of yarn in the center with another piece of yarn (figure 3). Cut the loops open on each end and fluff (figure 4). Stitch the warm fuzzy pompom to the top of the hat.

Mittens

Materials

- **Striped sweater, felted**
- **Scissors**
- **Needle and hand-quilting thread**
- **Large tapestry needle**
- **Knitting worsted yarn (approximately 2 ounces)**
- **Size 8 knitting needles**

Instructions

1 Refer to Making Mittens below to create your pattern. Do not extend the mitten pattern beyond your wrist for this project.

2 Lay the patterns on top of the sweater. Cut out two right-hand and two left-hand mittens without cuffs. Lay each mitten with right sides together and hand-stitch around the mitten, leaving the wrist area open.

3 Thread a tapestry needle with worsted-weight yarn. Sew with a blanket stitch around the edge of the wrist, making each stitch ¼" apart. See page 15 for stitch details.

4 To create the wristband, cast 24 stitches of knitting worsted yarn onto size 8 knitting needles. Knit 56 rows in garter stitch, creating 28 ridges. Compare the knitting to the mitten to see if you need more rows to match the distance around. Knit two to four more rows as needed and cast off. Hand-stitch the short ends together with the yarn.

5 Stitch the knitted wristband to the bottom of the mitten, by stitching through the blanket stitches.

6 Repeat steps 4 and 5 to make the second wristband and complete the other mitten.

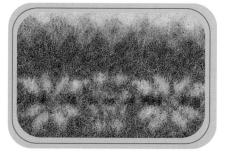

Making Mittens

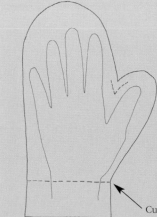

Cut here to add knitted cuffs.

Create a custom mitten pattern by drawing around the left or right hand on paper, adding 1" to the top of the fingers, and rounding the sides as shown. Draw a second line ¼" beyond the first outline for the seam allowance. Cut out the mitten pattern, trace it in reverse for the other hand, and cut out the second pattern.

To cut out mittens, lay the patterns on a felted sweater, aligning the bottom of the pattern with the ribbed edge of the sweater. Be sure to match any pattern and align stripes on the sweater, if necessary. Pin and cut out two left-hand mittens and two right-hand mittens, one layer at a time.

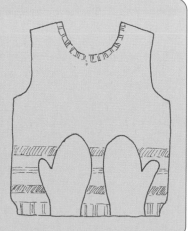

Ruby Slippers

I call these my ruby slippers, but whatever color yours are, when you slip them on your feet, you'll remember that "there's no place like home!"

Materials

Red sweater, felted

Scissors

Needle and red hand-quilting thread

Pins

Instructions

1. Make your pattern by tracing the slipper patterns on pages 118 and 120. Fold the sole pattern in half lengthwise and mark the center front and back.

2. Cut two slipper soles, one right slipper top, and one left slipper top from the red sweater. (Flip the right slipper top pattern over to cut the left slipper top.) Cut four 1½" x 4" strips of felted red sweater for the straps.

   Note: I can usually cut one slipper top from the sweater front and one from the back. I cut one sole from each sleeve.

3. Sew the center back seam on each slipper top. Lay the slipper top on the slipper sole, right sides together, and pin in place, matching the center fronts and center backs. Stitch and trim the seams close to the stitching. Whipstitch around the seams.

4. To create the straps, roll each of the 1½" x 4" strips lengthwise and whipstitch the outside raw edge. Crisscross two strips over a slipper and pin in place. To stitch the straps in place, remove the pins on one strap end and hold the strap against the slipper edge as you hand-stitch it to the slipper. Repeat for the other straps.

Another Option

For a different look, don't turn the slippers right side out after stitching the seams. Trim the seams to ⅛" and they will create a design element on the outside of the slippers.

Fingerless Hand-and-Wrist Warmers

This is an easy project that makes a great gift for crafters. As someone who loves to knit, sew, and generally make things, I have found that wrist warmers help me create in comfort. Plus, they make me feel very chic!

Materials

Dark rose sweater, felted
Scissors
Needle and hand-quilting thread
Pin

Instructions

1 Cut two 9"-long sleeves off of the sweater (figure 1). Fold down the cut edge ½" to the inside and hand-stitch in place to make a nicely finished edge. Repeat with the second sleeve.

2 Slide the fingerless mittens onto your hands, pinch the material between your thumb and forefinger, and mark this spot with a pin. This helps ensure that where you stitch them together is the most comfortable place.

3 Make a few small stitches at the point that you marked, stitching the front and back of the hand-and-wrist warmers together and creating a space for your thumb to slide through.

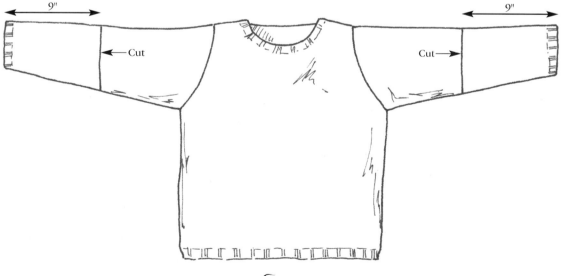

9"   9"

← Cut   Cut →

Figure 1

Lined Slippers

These lined slippers make toasty toes on cooler days. For a nice touch, sew some vintage silver buttons to the top center of each slipper. For the pink slippers, I used a cable-patterned felted sweater and omitted the buttons.

Materials

Medium to large felted sweater

Scissors

⅜ yard satin lining fabric

Needle and hand-quilting thread

Pins

2 vintage buttons (optional)

Instructions

1 Make patterns by tracing the slipper sole and slipper top patterns on pages 118 and 120.

2 Cut out two soles from the felted sweater, two soles from satin lining fabric, two slipper tops from felted fabric, and two slipper tops from lining fabric. Flip the right slipper top pattern over to cut the left slipper top.

Note: I can usually cut one slipper top from the sweater front and one from the back. I cut one sole from each sleeve.

3 Lay each slipper sole section onto a lining sole section, right sides together, and stitch around the outside edge, leaving a 3" opening to turn right side out (figure 1). Clip curves and turn right side out. Stitch the opening closed. Press.

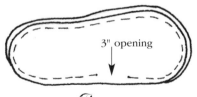

3" opening

Figure 1

4 Lay each slipper top section onto a lining section and stitch right sides together, leaving one center back edge open for turning. Stitch around the other center back seam. Clip the curves, turn right side out, and press. Turn the raw edges from the remaining center back seam under ¼" to the inside and whipstitch this opening closed.

5 On each slipper top, bring the center back sections together and whipstitch the two finished seams together so that the edges butt up against each other. Sew the center back seam on each slipper top.

6 Lay the slipper top on the slipper sole, right sides together, and pin in place, matching center fronts and center backs. Use plenty of pins, one every ¾" or so. Whipstitch the slipper tops to the slipper bottoms around the outside edge using hand-quilting thread. As you stitch the top to the bottom, this seam will become nearly invisible.

7 Embellish with vintage buttons, if desired.

Use Your Scraps

Slipper lining can be made from almost any satiny or soft material—an old dress, a discarded cotton bedspread, even the satin pirate pants your child wore in the school play.

Bolero Angora Sweater

Recently, I saw a very pricey sweater similar to this in a trendy magazine. Considering that my sweater and yard-sale brooch cost only a few dollars, and it took me about 30 minutes of work, I got quite the bargain! Since this sweater is felted, the cut edges will not ravel and do not require hemming. Wear this sweater over your favorite T-shirt, securing it with a rhinestone brooch.

Materials

Black angora sweater, felted

Pins

Chalk marker

Scissors

Vintage rhinestone brooch

Note: A slipover sweater is easiest for this project. Be sure to start with a sweater that's much larger than the desired size.

Instructions

1 Mark the center front of the sweater with a pin. With a chalk marker, start at the top shoulder seam of the sweater and draw a rounded line to the center pin, rounding down back toward the side seams of the sweater (figure 1). Try on the sweater to see whether the chalk markings fall in the right places for you, and adjust them if necessary.

2 Cut along the chalk line on one side of the sweater. Lay the cut side down on the uncut side of the sweater and pin in place for a guideline. Mark this area with chalk and cut along the chalk line. Cut the sweater back straight across so that it is even with the bottom edge of the sweater front. Secure the sweater with a rhinestone brooch.

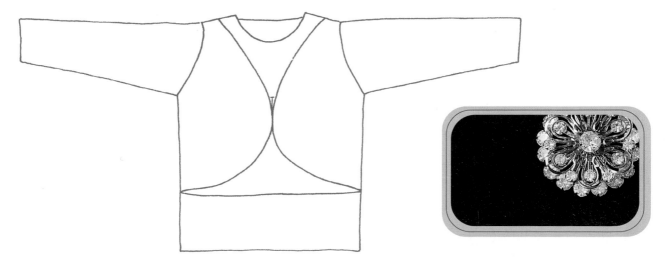

Figure 1

Romantic Scarf

Ah, romance! If you love roses and lace and snuggling on cold days, this scarf is for you.
It really sets the mood with clusters of roses just blossoming with possibilities.

Materials

Sage green sweater, felted

Scissors

Needle and hand-quilting thread

Sewing machine (optional)

File folder, cardstock, or template plastic

Chalk marker

18" (½ yard) vintage crocheted trim

Felting needle and foam pad

Wool roving: 3 shades of rose, 2 shades of green, yellow, and brown

Chalk Transfer

Light boxes and windows will not help too much when it comes to tracing pattern designs onto thick felted wool. Aside from drawing the pattern freehand, here's a method that I have used.

1. Trace the pattern onto paper and then rub a piece of colored chalk on the back of the paper pattern. Rub the paper lightly with a facial tissue to remove excess chalk.

2. Place the pattern drawn side up and chalk side down on the felted sweater fabric. Draw over the pattern guidelines firmly with a pen or stylus. When you remove the pattern, you should have a nice chalk outline. If not, rub more chalk onto the paper and repeat.

Remember to use light-colored chalk for a dark sweater and dark-colored chalk for a lighter sweater. You should be able to rub or brush off the chalk when you are finished if it still shows.

Instructions

1 To create the scarf, cut off the sweater sleeves, cut open the seams, and lay the fabric flat. Cut the sweater into 7½"-wide sections until you have enough to make the scarf the length you prefer, anywhere from 44" to 72" long.

2 Trim the sweater pieces on the diagonal and butt the raw edges together. Be sure to use ribbed edges on each end of the scarf. Stitch them together by machine using a zigzag stitch or whipstitch by hand.

3 Make a template of the scallop pattern on page 122 using a file folder, cardstock, or template plastic. Mark around the edge of the template with a chalk marker to create the scalloped edges on the scarf. Cut along the marked line with your best scissors for a nice, clean edge.

4 Stitch the vintage crochet trim to each end.

Vintage Trims

Vintage crocheted trims are inexpensive and are usually found in antique stores or yard sales. You can also collect wonderful crocheted trims from old nightgowns, bedcovers, or pillowcases. Cut the trim from the article, fold it over, and hand-stitch any edges that may need hemming.

5 To transfer the needle-felting pattern onto the scarf, use a chalk marker and draw the design freehand, using the patterns on pages 122 and 123 as a guide. If you prefer, transfer the design by using the method described in Chalk Transfer on this page.

6 Once the designs are drawn onto the scarf, place one area on the foam pad and use the felting needle to punch small wisps of wool roving in place on the design. Follow the instructions in Needle Felting on page 18.

7 Add the color in layers, with brown for the stems and tendrils and green as an accent. For the leaves, begin with dark green roving, then add a layer of light green and some yellow highlights. For the flowers, add dark rose wool roving in the basic circle shape, wisps of medium rose wool roving for circular accents, and some lighter rose wool roving for the small round centers. When the needle felting is done, wrap the scarf around your neck and head out for a romantic evening!

Creative Companions: Charming Go-Togethers and Duos

"Whatever you can do or dream you can begin it!
Boldness has genius, power, and magic in it."

—GOETHE

Newton's Laws of Motion tell us that a body at rest tends to remain at rest, and a body in motion tends to remain in motion. When you are involved in a creative activity, sometimes you just can't stop being creative. You go on to make something else and surprise yourself. You begin a pair of mittens, and before you know it you've made a matching scarf with the leftover fabric. Start a fanciful hat and find how easy it is to whip out some leg warmers. Getting started on one project can lead to the discovery of its creative companion, just waiting in the wings.

Snowy Days Set

Here's another addition for keeping little bodies warm. This scarf is a great creative companion to the mittens, but you can also use it on your snowman for some frosty fun. The mittens will keep small hands warm and dry while building that snowman.

Scarf

Materials

Solid colored sweater, felted

Patterned sweater with ribbing, felted

Scissors

Pins

Needle and hand-quilting thread

Ivory bulky yarn

Crochet hook

Instructions

1 Cut five 3½" x 7" rectangles from the solid felted sweater. Cut two 4½" x 7" rectangles and two 3½" x 7" rectangles from the patterned felted sweater.

2 Cut off the sweater sleeves from the patterned sweater, cut open the seams, and lay the fabric flat. Cut two 7" x 9" rectangles from the patterned sweater sleeves, with ribbing along the 7" end.

3 Pin the 7" side of a 7" x 9" rectangle of patterned fabric to the 7" side of a solid-colored rectangle, right sides together. Alternate the solid and patterned rectangles, ending with a 7" x 9" rectangle (figure 1). When all the rectangles are pinned, stitch them together and trim the seams.

4 Fold the scarf in half lengthwise, right sides together, and stitch along the long outside edges. Turn right side out and press.

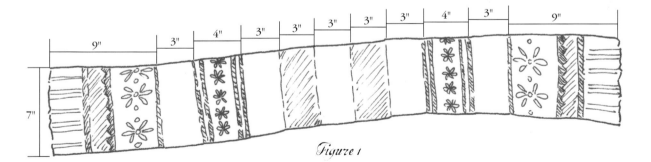

Figure 1

Save Some for Later

When cutting out the pieces for these projects, you might want to cut the mittens first. Then use the sleeves and other scraps for the scarf.

93

5 To create the fringe, cut the yarn into twenty-eight 12" strips. Gently insert the small crochet hook through the bottom edge of the ribbing about ¼" from the edge. Fold each yarn piece in half and place the loop onto the crochet hook (figure 2). Pull the crochet hook back through the ribbing, partially pulling the loop through (figure 3). Thread the two loose yarn ends through the loop and pull them tightly to make each piece of fringe. Continue in this manner to add 14 lengths of fringe to each end of the scarf. Trim as desired.

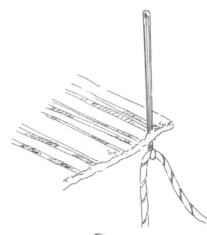

Figure 2

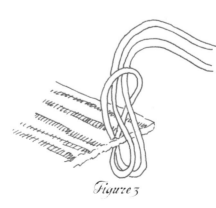

Figure 3

Mittens

Materials

Patterned sweater with ribbing, felted

Scissors

Needle and hand-quilting thread

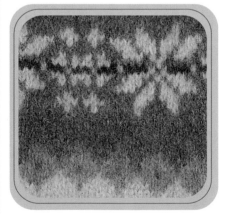

Instructions

1 See Making Mittens on page 79 to create a custom mitten pattern.

2 Lay out the pattern with the bottom of the mittens along the ribbed edge of the sweater. Cut two right-hand and two left-hand mittens from the felted fabric, matching stripes or other patterns as needed.

3 Lay the mittens right sides together, and stitch ¼" around the edges, leaving them open at the wrists. Trim ⅛" from the edges and turn right side out.

Victorian Scarf and Mittens

Victorian Scarf and Mittens

Every so often I need to create something dripping with ribbons and lace, and this scarf and mitten set really satisfies that urge. Start with a few wool sweaters in yummy plum and lavender colors, add a large vintage lacy doily, and tie them together with a few rows of luscious knitted ribbon . . . a delicious combination!

Scarf

Materials

Dark plum sweater with ribbing, felted

Ribbing from lavender felted sweater

Scissors

Needle and hand-quilting thread

Sewing machine (optional)

Size 30 knitting needles

20 yards ⅝"-wide plum ribbon

⅓ yard flat lace (optional)

12"-diameter round lace doily

1 yard 1¼"-wide green ribbon

Instructions

1 From the plum felted sweater, cut enough 5"-wide strips to make a 5" x 50" scarf. From the lavender sweater ribbing, cut three 3" x 12" strips.

2 Hand-stitch the 5"-wide strips of plum fabric together, butting the raw edges along the 5" sides to make a 5" x 50" scarf. You can also use a sewing machine to zigzag-stitch the sections together.

3 Using the knitting needles and the plum ribbon, cast on 15 stitches and knit 6 rows of garter-stitch, creating a 4½" x 5"-wide row of knitting. Cast off. Repeat to create an identical knitted section for the other end of the scarf. Hand-stitch one knitted section to each end of the scarf. Note: If you prefer not to knit, cut the scarf a few inches longer and add a section of flat lace purchased from your local fabric store.

Save Some for Later

When cutting out the pieces for this project, save the lower portion of the dark plum sweater with the ribbed bottom for the Victorian Mittens.

Figure 1

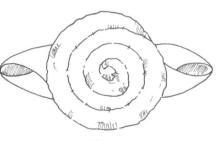

Figure 2

Figure 3

4 Cut the lace doily in half. Run a hand-gathering stitch along the cut edges and pull the gathers to make two 5"-wide strips. Stitch a doily to each end of the scarf.

5 Make three Rolled Victorian Roses from the lavender ribbing strips following the instructions on page 26, but do not create the leaves. Instead, create leaves by cutting the green ribbon into five 7" lengths. Fold each section in half, overlapping the ends (figure 1). Run a hand-gathering stitch along the overlapped section and pull tightly to secure. Tuck the leaves behind the flowers and tack in place (figure 2). Arrange the flowers on the scarf and tack in place (figure 3).

Nearly Invisible Seams

When making scarves, it's easy to connect felted fabric sections together, especially if you're machine sewing. Align the straight edges and zigzag-stitch them together where the edges meet. If you're hand stitching, you can make a nearly invisible seam by aligning the straight edges and whipstitching, catching only the top fibers of the fabric. Turn the fabric over and whipstitch the bottom. The sections will seem to melt together as if they were knit that way.

Mittens

Materials

Dark plum sweater with ribbing, felted
Ribbing from lavender sweater, felted
Scissors
Needle and hand-quilting thread
Sewing machine (optional)
5"-diameter round lace doily
20" length of 1¼"-wide green ribbon

Instructions

1 Create a custom mitten pattern by following the instructions in Making Mittens on page 79.

2 Lay out the pattern with the bottom of the mittens along the ribbed edging of the plum felted sweater. Cut two right-hand and two left-hand mittens from the sweater. Cut two 2" x 8" strips of lavender felted ribbing.

3 Lay the mittens right sides together, and stitch ¼" around the edge, by hand or by machine. Leave the mittens open at the wrists. Trim ¼" from the seam allowances and turn right side out.

4 Cut a 5"-diameter doily in half. Stitch half the doily to the front of each mitten as shown in the photo.

5 Using the lavender ribbing, make four Rolled Victorian Roses (page 26), but do not make the leaves. Instead, create leaves by cutting the ribbon into 5" lengths. Run a hand-gathering stitch across the center of the ribbon and pull to gather. Tuck the leaves behind the flowers and tack in place. Arrange the roses on the mittens as shown and tack in place over the lace doily.

Aran Isle Tote Bag and Eyeglass Case

This bag was made from a beautiful Aran sweater that my friend Jeannine O'Grady bought for me in Ireland more than ten years ago. The sweater somehow made its way into my washer and to my dismay, felted itself. I couldn't bear to part with it and saved it in a drawer for years. I was thrilled to be able to finally have a way to use this "shrunken treasure," and it's become my favorite bag to take to the beach, the park, or the knitting circle.

Tote

Materials

- Aran Isle sweater, felted
- Chalk marker
- Scissors
- Needle and hand-quilting thread
- 1 yard lining fabric
- 4" diameter plastic canvas circle
- Pins
- Vintage button
- 10" length of ivory wool yarn

Instructions

1 Mark a line across the sweater below the underarms (figure 1). Cut along this line. Cut off the sweater sleeves, cut open the seams, and lay the fabric flat.

Note: Measure the width and length of the purse front and back so you will know what size to cut your lining later on.

2 For the straps, use the remaining sweater sections to cut enough 4"-wide strips to make two 4" x 40" strips (figures 1 and 2). Cut a 5"-diameter circle from one sleeve edge. Be sure to leave an 8½" square section with ribbing from the sleeve if you plan to make the eyeglass case.

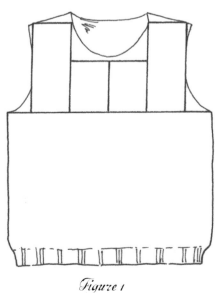

Figure 1

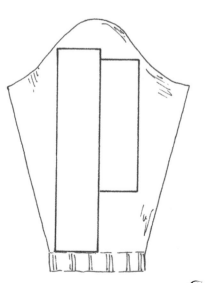

Figure 2

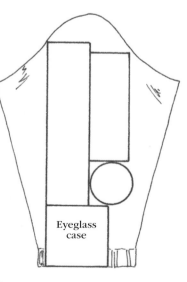

Eyeglass case

3 Stitch the 4" strips together along the 4" edges to make two 40"-long straps.

4 Cut two 4" x 40" strips from the lining fabric. Lay the lining against the felted straps with right sides together and stitch along each long side ¼" from the edge. Trim the seam and turn right side out. Press the straps with an iron. Turn the ends under and stitch.

5 Topstitch ½" in from the strap edge along each side to stabilize the edges and create a finished look.

6 To make the purse bottom, run a hand-gathering stitch around the 5"-diameter felted sweater circle and pull up the gathers slightly. Place the plastic canvas circle inside the 5"-diameter felted circle and pull up tightly on the threads (figure 3). Stitch to secure.

7 Run a hand-gathering stitch around the bottom edge of the purse and pull up the gathers (figures 4 and 5). Center and pin the felted circle (with the plastic canvas inside) to the bottom of the purse and hand-stitch in place (figure 6).

8 Cut a purse lining the same dimensions as the purse body. Cut a 5"-diameter lining circle. Stitch the side seams of the purse lining with right sides together, leaving an open (unstitched) area along one long side seam. Run a hand-gathering stitch along the bottom edge of the lining and pull up the gathers tightly. Center the gathers around the lining circle and pin. Stitch the lining to the circle, using a ¼" seam.

9 Turn the purse lining inside out and lay the purse body inside the lining, right sides together. Pin the top edges of the purse and lining together and stitch completely around the top edge. Pull the purse right side out through the side opening of the lining and then hand-stitch the lining closed.

10 Pin the straps to the purse on both sides and whip-stitch in place.

11 Hand-stitch a vintage button to the center top of the bag. Fold the length of yarn in half to create a loop and tie a knot 2" from the center fold. Stitch to the back of the purse so that the yarn will loop over the button. Wrap the excess ends of the yarn into a little spiral with your fingers and stitch it down onto the back of the purse.

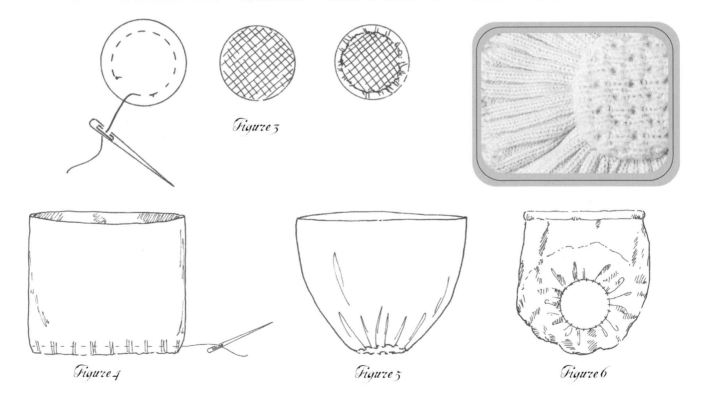

Figure 3

Figure 4

Figure 5

Figure 6

Eyeglass Case

Materials

One 8½" square of felted Aran Isle sweater with ribbing

Needle and hand-quilting thread

Scissors

Sewing machine (optional)

Vintage button

Instructions

1 Fold the 8½" square of felted fabric in half with right sides together and stitch around three sides (including the folded edge), leaving the ribbed edge open. Trim the seams and machine-sew them with a zigzag stitch for a nice finish, if desired.

2 Turn right side out and stitch a vintage button to the top front.

Collect Classic Sweaters

I always snap up classic sweaters such as Aran Isle knits and argyle vests and sweaters. I never pass up black, gray, or red sweaters either.

Warm-As-a-Hug Wrap and Handbag

Every woman needs an elegant purse for her theater tickets, lipstick, fine perfume, and a piece of her favorite chocolate. This one fills the bill perfectly and is exquisite when paired with the Warm-As-a-Hug Wrap.

Handbag

Materials

Sleeves from an extra-large, hip-length sweater, felted or unfelted

Scissors

Needle and hand-quilting thread

⅓ yard satin lining fabric

Pins

3⅓-yard length (120") of 1½"-wide sheer ribbon

24" length of 1½"-wide sheer ribbon

Instructions

1 Cut two purse sections from the sweater sleeves, enlarging the pattern on page 117 (figure 1). From the remainder, cut three 2" x 10" strips for roses and seven leaves, using the pattern on page 108.

2 Lay the two purse sections right sides together, and stitch around the bottom and sides, leaving the top open.

3 Cut two purse linings from the satin fabric using the purse pattern. Lay the two purse linings right sides together, and stitch around the bottom and sides, leaving the top open and a 5" opening along one side.

4 Turn the lining right side out and press. Slide the lining inside the purse, right sides together. Pin the top edges of the purse and lining together and stitch completely around the top edge. Pull the purse right side out through the side opening of the lining, and then hand-stitch the lining closed. Press and topstitch ⅝" away from the top edge.

5 To make the purse strap, cut one 2" x 40" strip of satin fabric. Fold the fabric in half right sides together to make a 1" x 40" strap. Stitch around two sides, leaving one short edge open. Turn right side out.

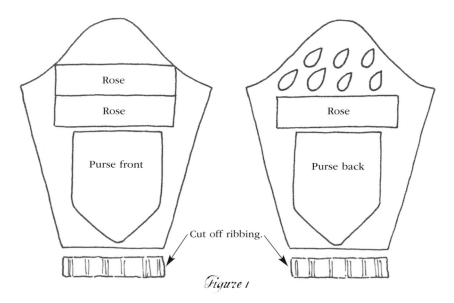

Rose

Rose

Purse front

Rose

Purse back

Cut off ribbing.

Figure 1

6 Fold the 120" length of ribbon in half so that it is 60" long, and stitch the edges together ⅛" from each long edge to make a casing. Slide the purse strap into this casing and stitch one end to secure the lining to the casing. Scrunch up the ribbon over the satin strap until the ends meet, to create gathers in the ribbon casing. Stitch the ends closed. Stitch one end of the strap to each side of the purse.

7 Make three Rolled Victorian Roses (page 26) using the 2" x 10" sweater strips. Arrange the roses across the top front of the bag along with the seven leaves, and then hand-stitch in place.

8 Add a 4" bow made from the 24" length of ribbon and tuck it under the roses. Tack it in place.

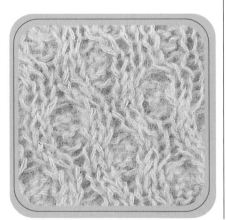

Wrap

Materials

Extra-large, hip-length mohair or angora sweater with ribbing, felted or unfelted

Scissors

Needle and all-purpose thread

24" length of 1½"-wide sheer pink ribbon

1"-diameter glass button

Instructions

1 Cut 10" off the bottom of the sweater through both thicknesses (figure 1). Be sure to leave the sweater side seams intact. The ribbed edge will be the top of the wrap. Cut a 5" slit on the bottom front section of the felted fabric about 8" from one side of the sweater.

2 Fold the 5" cut edges under about ¼" and hand-stitch to hem the opening. Fold the bottom edge of the wrap under ½" and hand-stitch a hem to finish the edges.

3 Create a 4" bow from the sheer ribbon. Tack it in place just above the slit and attach a button to the bow.

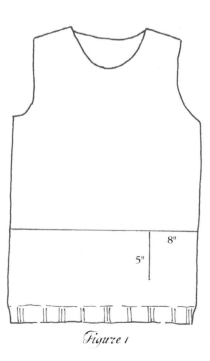

8"

5"

Figure 1

This beret has an earthy yet trendy look that I love. Pair it with the leg warmers, and you're ready for any adventure in the cool autumn air. I jokingly call it my "dinner plate special" because I used a dinner plate and a dessert saucer to get perfect circles for the beret.

Leg Warmers

Materials

Sleeves from an extra-large tweed sweater, felted

Scissors

Chalk marker

Felting needle and foam pad

Wool roving: light and dark rose; green

Needle and hand-quilting thread

Instructions

1 Cut open the seams of the sweater sleeves and lay the fabric flat (figure 1). Cut straight across the sleeves at the widest point.

2 To embellish the leg warmers, use a chalk marker to draw the design onto the sweater sleeve just above the ribbing. Draw it freehand using the pattern on page 119 or see Chalk Transfer on page 89.

3 Place the sleeve onto the foam pad, arrange the wool roving in small wisps along the outline of the design, and needle felt in place. For the roses, twist a light rose and a dark rose length of roving together as for the beret (figure 2 on page 107). The twists should be about the length and width of a standard pencil. Roll the twists into a spiral and tack in place with the felting needle.

4 Fold the leg warmer in half, right sides together, and re-stitch the seam. Turn right side out.

5 Turn the top edge of each leg warmer down ½" and hand-stitch in place to hem.

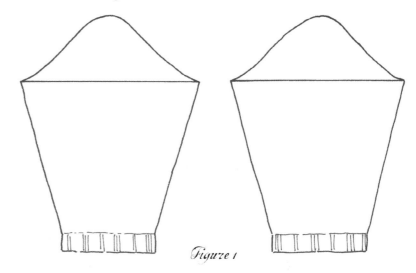

Figure 1

Beret

Materials

Extra-large brown tweed sweater, felted

Scissors

Chalk marker

Felting needle and foam pad

Wool roving: light and dark rose,
   light and dark green

Large embroidery needle and
   embroidery floss

Pins

Instructions

1 Cut two 11" diameter circles from the body of the sweater. Cut a 5"-diameter hole in the center of one of the circles (figure 1).

2 Use a chalk marker to draw the design onto the circle with the hole in the center. Draw it free-hand using the pattern on page 119, or see Chalk Transfer on page 89. Place the marked hat bottom onto the foam pad.

3 Arrange the wool roving in small wisps along the outline of the design, and needle felt in place. For the roses, twist a light rose and a dark rose length of roving together (figure 2). The twists should be about the length and width of a standard pencil. Roll the twists into a spiral and tack in place with the felting needle.

4 To finish the hat, thread six strands of embroidery floss onto the embroidery needle, and blanket-stitch around the inside circle of the hat bottom. Lay the hat top and bottom with wrong sides together and pin around the edge. Blanket-stitch the edges of the hat together, using six strands of embroidery floss.

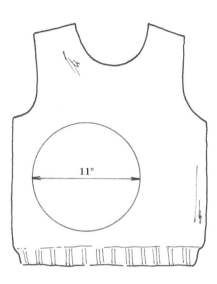

11"

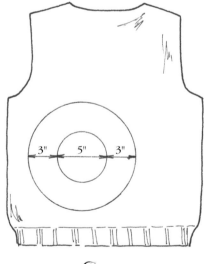

3" 5" 3"

Figure 1

Figure 2

Patterns

Angora Ribbing Rose with Bud
Rolled Victorian Roses
Serendipity Rose

Ivory Angora Rose
Serendipity Rose
Warm-as-a-Hug Handbag

Leaf Pattern

Leaf Pattern

Twisty Lollipop Rose

Leaf Pattern

Pretty Posies
Over-the-Shoulder Bag

Pretty Posies

Leaf Pattern

Large Petal Pattern

Small Petal Pattern

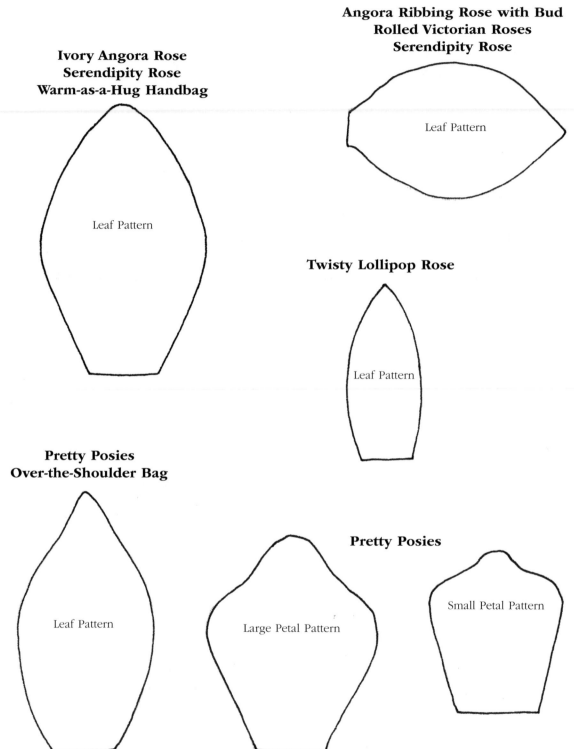

Serendipity Rose Pins

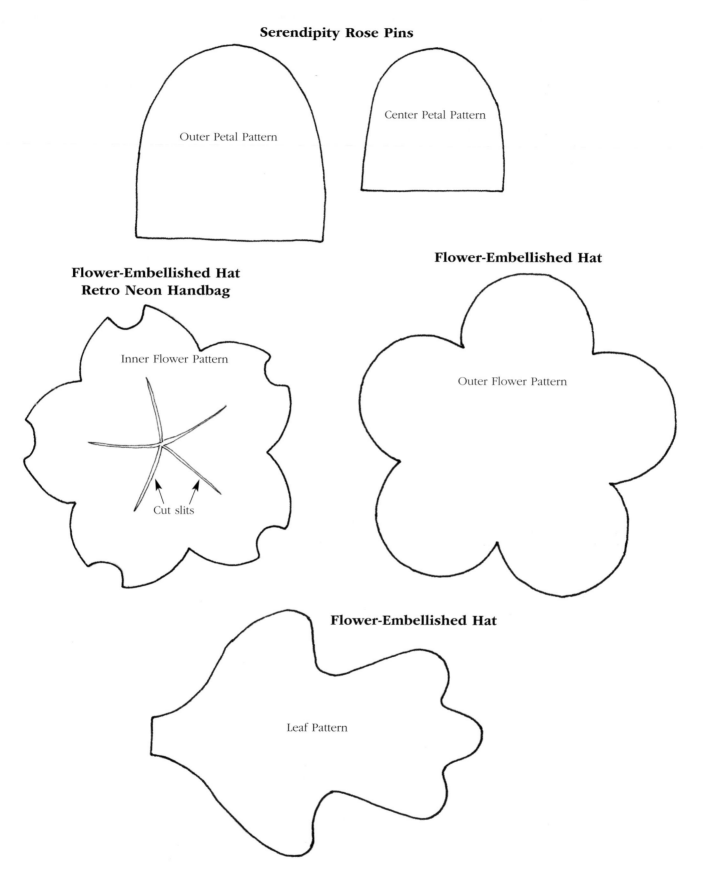

Outer Petal Pattern

Center Petal Pattern

Flower-Embellished Hat
Retro Neon Handbag

Inner Flower Pattern

Cut slits

Flower-Embellished Hat

Outer Flower Pattern

Flower-Embellished Hat

Leaf Pattern

109

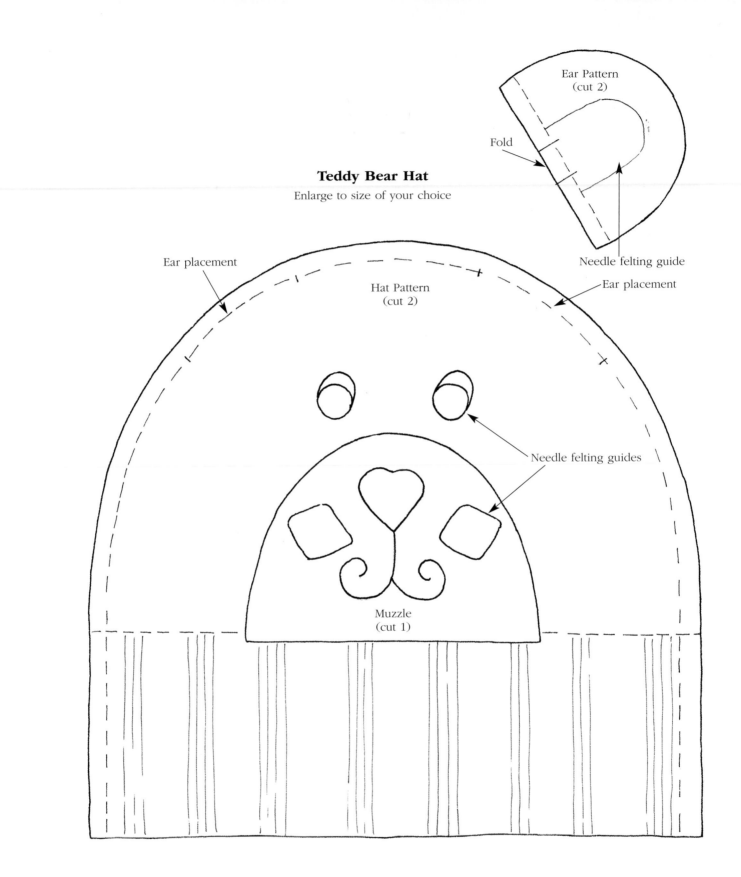

Ear Pattern
(cut 2)

Fold

Needle felting guide

Teddy Bear Hat

Enlarge to size of your choice

Ear placement

Ear placement

Hat Pattern
(cut 2)

Needle felting guides

Muzzle
(cut 1)

Elf Boots
Enlarge to size of your choice

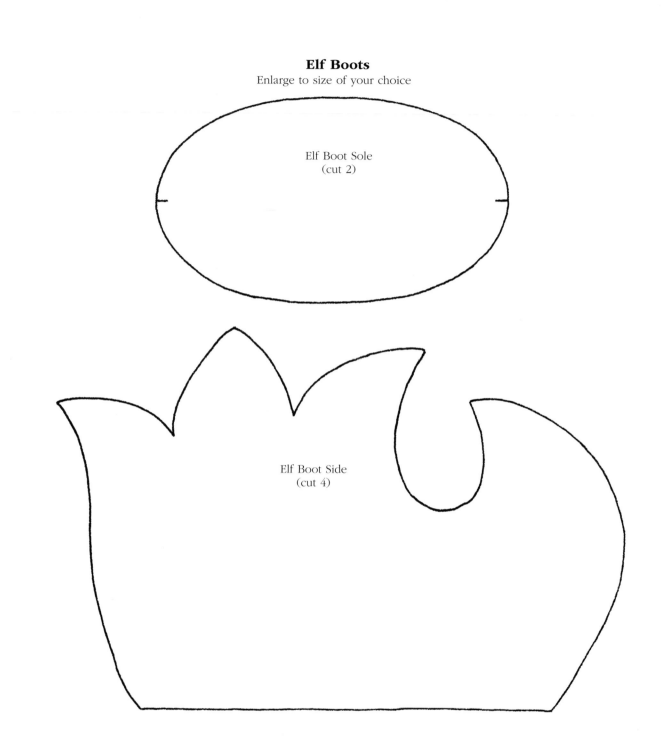

Elf Boot Sole
(cut 2)

Elf Boot Side
(cut 4)

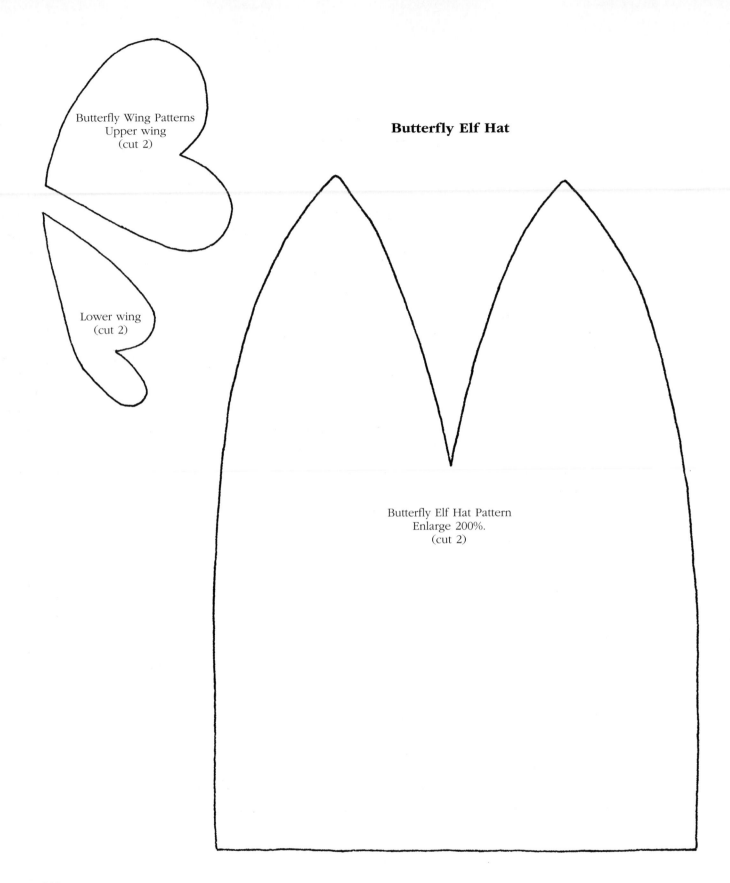

Butterfly Wing Patterns
Upper wing
(cut 2)

Lower wing
(cut 2)

Butterfly Elf Hat

Butterfly Elf Hat Pattern
Enlarge 200%.
(cut 2)

Elf Ball

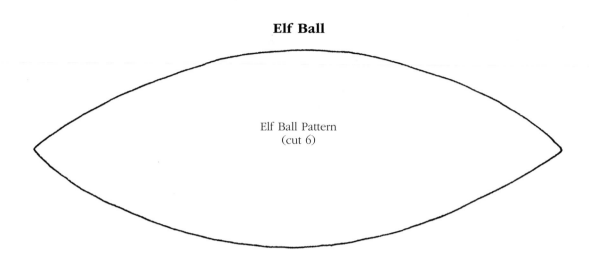

Elf Ball Pattern
(cut 6)

Day to Evening Shoulder Pack

Enlarge to size of your choice.

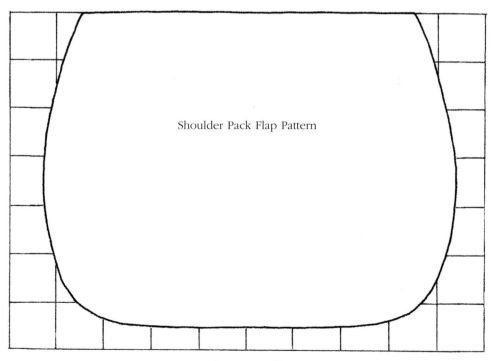

Shoulder Pack Flap Pattern

1 square = 1"

Sweet Angora Bunny

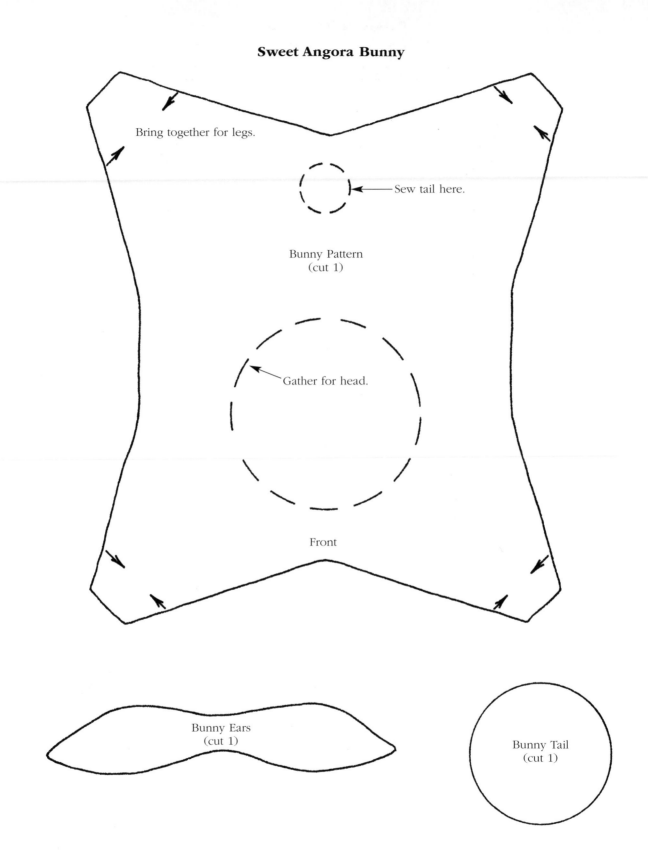

Bring together for legs.

Sew tail here.

Bunny Pattern
(cut 1)

Gather for head.

Front

Bunny Ears
(cut 1)

Bunny Tail
(cut 1)

Basket of Roses Purse

Enlarge to size of your choice.

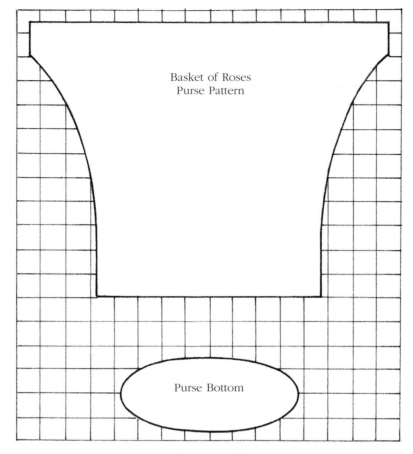

Basket of Roses
Purse Pattern

Purse Bottom

1 square = 1"

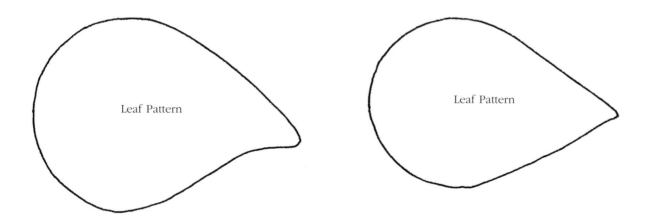

Leaf Pattern

Leaf Pattern

Little Girl's Hat with Daisy

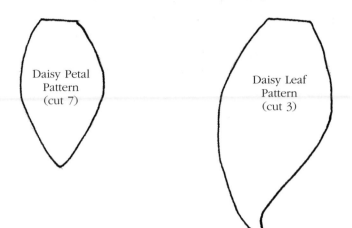

Daisy Petal
Pattern
(cut 7)

Daisy Leaf
Pattern
(cut 3)

Winter Wonderland Set

Winter Wonderland Set

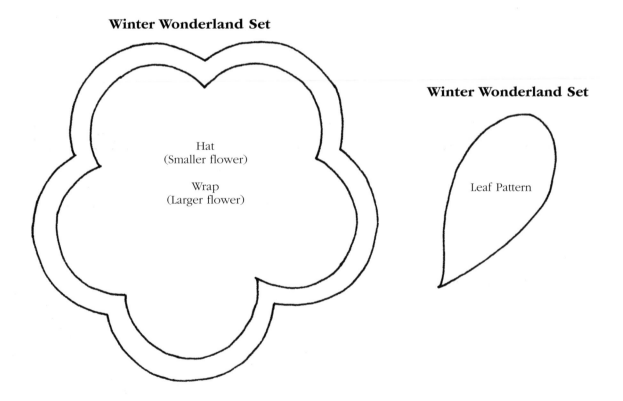

Hat
(Smaller flower)

Wrap
(Larger flower)

Leaf Pattern

Warm Fuzzy Hat

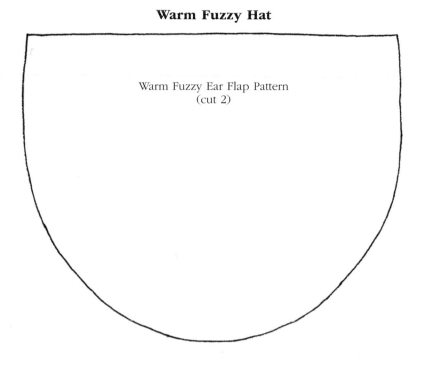

Warm Fuzzy Ear Flap Pattern
(cut 2)

Warm-as-a-Hug Handbag

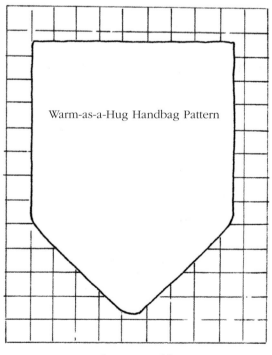

Warm-as-a-Hug Handbag Pattern

1 square = 1"

Retro Neon Handbag

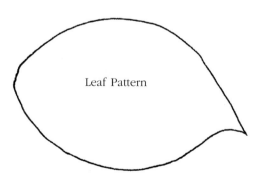

Leaf Pattern

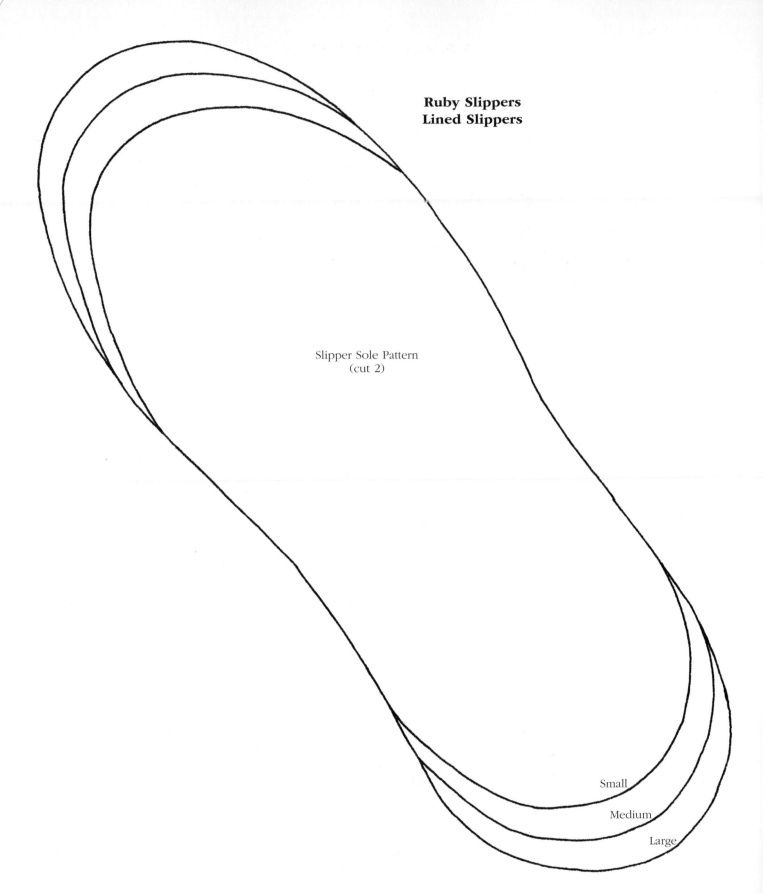

Ruby Slippers
Lined Slippers

Slipper Sole Pattern
(cut 2)

Small

Medium

Large

A Touch of Paris Beret Set

Touch of Paris Beret
Needle Felting Pattern

Enlarge 200%

A Touch of Paris Leg Warmers
Needle Felting Pattern

Ruby Slippers
Lined Slippers

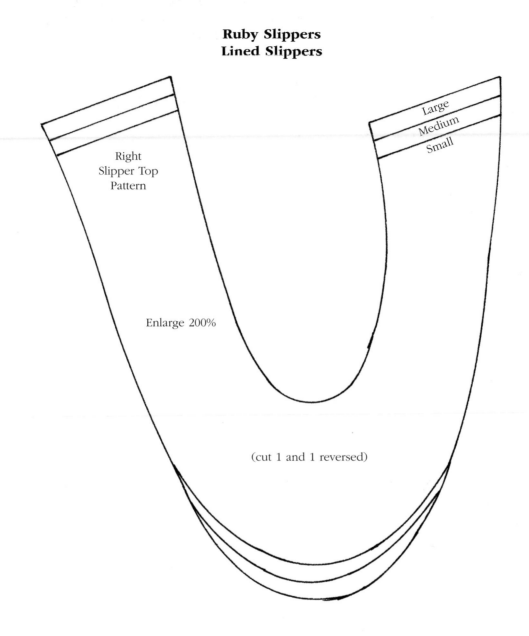

Large
Medium
Small

Right
Slipper Top
Pattern

Enlarge 200%

(cut 1 and 1 reversed)

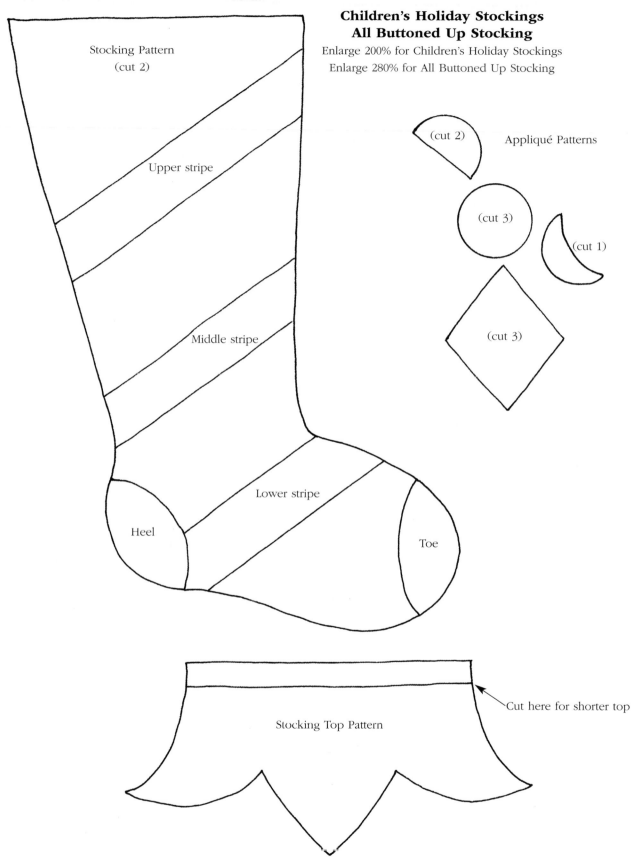

**Children's Holiday Stockings
All Buttoned Up Stocking**

Enlarge 200% for Children's Holiday Stockings

Enlarge 280% for All Buttoned Up Stocking

Stocking Pattern
(cut 2)

Upper stripe

Middle stripe

Lower stripe

Heel

Toe

(cut 2)

Appliqué Patterns

(cut 3)

(cut 1)

(cut 3)

Cut here for shorter top

Stocking Top Pattern

121

Romantic Scarf
Needle Felting Pattern

Scallop Pattern

122

Metric Conversion Chart

INCHES	METRIC (MM/CM)	INCHES	METRIC (MM/CM)	INCHES	METRIC (MM/CM)
1/8	3 mm	8 1/2	21.6 cm	23	58.4 cm
3/16	5 mm	9	22.9 cm	23 1/2	59.7 cm
1/4	6 mm	9 1/2	24.1 cm	24	61 cm
5/16	8 mm	10	25.4 cm	24 1/2	62.2 cm
3/8	9.5 mm	10 1/2	26.7 cm	25	63.5 cm
7/16	1.1 cm	11	27.9 cm	25 1/2	64.8 cm
1/2	1.3 cm	11 1/2	29.2 cm	26	66 cm
9/16	1.4 cm	12	30.5 cm	26 1/2	67.3 cm
5/8	1.6 cm	12 1/2	31.8 cm	27	68.6 cm
11/16	1.7 cm	13	33 cm	27 1/2	69.9 cm
3/4	1.9 cm	13 1/2	34.3 cm	28	71.1 cm
13/16	2.1 cm	14	35.6 cm	28 1/2	72.4 cm
7/8	2.2 cm	14 1/2	36.8 cm	29	73.7 cm
15/16	2.4 cm	15	38.1 cm	29 1/2	74.9 cm
1	2.5 cm	15 1/2	39.4 cm	30	76.2 cm
1 1/2	3.8 cm	16	40.6 cm	30 1/2	77.5 cm
2	5 cm	16 1/2	41.9 cm	31	78.7 cm
2 1/2	6.4 cm	17	43.2 cm	31 1/2	80 cm
3	7.6 cm	17 1/2	44.5 cm	32	81.3 cm
3 1/2	8.9 cm	18	45.7 cm	32 1/2	82.6 cm
4	10.2 cm	18 1/2	47 cm	33	83.8 cm
4 1/2	11.4 cm	19	48.3 cm	33 1/2	85 cm
5	12.7 cm	19 1/2	49.5 cm	34	86.4 cm
5 1/2	14 cm	20	50.8 cm	34 1/2	87.6 cm
6	15.2 cm	20 1/2	52 cm	35	88.9 cm
6 1/2	16.5 cm	21	53.3 cm	35 1/2	90.2 cm
7	17.8 cm	21 1/2	54.6 cm	36	91.4 cm
7 1/2	19 cm	22	55 cm	36 1/2	92.7 cm
8	20.3 cm	22 1/2	57.2 cm	37	94.0 cm

Acknowledgments

I would like to thank . . .

Jo Packham, for inspiring and delighting me for many years with her laughter, friendship, creative vision, and love of exquisitely unique people and designs.

Barbara Milburn, for encouraging me when I first whispered the idea for this book to her and for having a kind voice and a warm heart.

My husband, Roban, for loving me through each and every adventure, "Come what may."

My five creative and brilliant children—Rileigh, Jason, Katelyn, Skylar, and Tristan.

My parents, Dale and Joan Tidwell, whose example taught me how to live a creative and joyful life.

My father-in-law and mother-in-law, Bob and Carol Bieber, for their constant love and support.

My brothers and sisters, who have each taught me wonderful things, with special thanks to Allyson for driving me all over Utah to collect sweaters for this book, and to Sue for being on a constant search for those elusive argyle sweaters!

My friend and sister Gretchen Bieber for being a rainbow and reminding me about sunshine on those occasional cloudy days.

Ellen Pahl for being the best editor on the planet!

The Waldorf School of Santa Barbara, for awakening me to a whole new world of creativity that I had been searching for. Special thanks to the members of our Tuesday morning knitting circle, especially Alicia Dodge, for guiding Skylar and me down the knitting path in her Handwork class.

My Waldorf friends, who have been a constant source of inspiration on every level: Meg Butler, Heidi Debra, Lisa Gates, Ann Dusenberry, Maggie Rauen, Connie Manson Chinn, and the whole gang.

Cherry Field with a big hug for always believing in me!

The radiant Ivonne Delaflor, author and friend, for helping me remember who I am during difficult times and reminding me that we all have the power to create the life of our dreams!

Fred Mendelsohn, Dr. John Ott, Cynthia Bently-DeNight, and the good folks at Ott-Light Technology, for making it possible for me to express my creativity 24/7. I feel like I have a sunlit window over my craft table with the flip of a switch on my Ott-light. I really can't thank you enough.

Bernina of America, for sharing their amazing needle punch tool with me. Wow!

And to a great man, Spencer W. Kimball, whose words inspire me daily with this wonderful thought: "We must play the song we came on earth to play . . . Let us not die with our music still in us."

About the Author

"It is something to be able to paint a particular picture, or to carve a statue, and so to make a few objects beautiful; but it is far more glorious to carve and paint the very atmosphere and medium through which we look. To affect the quality of the day—that is the highest of arts."

—Henry David Thoreau

Katheryn Tidwell Bieber has been designing and creating as long as she can remember, and she learned from her parents the secrets of creative joy. Nationally known as host and craft designer for *Aleene's Creative Living* and other television shows, including *Home Matters, Our Place, Handmade by Design, America Sews,* and more, Katheryn always seems to be following a new creative muse. From ribbonwork to mosaics to scrapbooking, Katheryn has designed a wide variety of projects for companies such as Butterick, Simplicity, and Vogue, and for magazines, including *Better Homes and Gardens, McCall's, Family Circle, Woman's Day,* and more. A powerful motivational speaker, Katheryn speaks from the heart on the secrets of living a life filled with love and joy. She lives in Santa Barbara, California, with her husband and five children.

Katheryn can be reached at Katheryn@feltitstitchit.com or visit her website at feltitstitchit.com.

Index

Bieber, Katheryn
Tidwell.

Felt it! stitch it!
fabulous!

DATE			